The real long-term challenge

of the rise of China

CHINA RISING:

WILL THE WEST BE ABLE TO COPE?

World Scientific Series on 21st Century Business

ISSN: 1793-5660

World Scientific Series on
21st Century Business : 3

The real long-term challenge

of the rise of China

CHINA RISING:

WILL THE WEST BE ABLE TO COPE?

Jan Willem Blankert

World Scientific

JERSEY · LONDON · SINGAPORE · BEIJING · SHANGHAI · HONG KONG · TAIPEI · CHENNAI

Published by

World Scientific Publishing Co. Pte. Ltd.

5 Toh Tuck Link, Singapore 596224

USA office: 27 Warren Street, Suite 401-402, Hackensack, NJ 07601

UK office: 57 Shelton Street, Covent Garden, London WC2H 9HE

Library of Congress Cataloging-in-Publication Data
Blankert, Jan Willem.
    China rising : will the West be able to cope? : the real long-term challenge of the rise of China
and Asia in general / by Jan Willem Blankert.
        p. cm. -- (World scientific series on 21st century business ; vol. 3)
    Includes bibliographical references and index.
    ISBN-13 978-981-283-795-0
    ISBN-10 981-283-795-7
    1. China--Economic conditions--2000– 2. United States--Economic conditions--2001–
3. Competition, International. I. Title.
    HC427.95.B53 2009
    330.951--dc22
                                                                    2009015972

British Library Cataloguing-in-Publication Data
A catalogue record for this book is available from the British Library.

Typeset by Stallion Press
Email: enquiries@stallionpress.com

Printed in Singapore.

CHINA RISING: Will the West be Able to Cope?

The real long-term challenge of the rise of China — and Asia in general — is not about trade competition, investment, jobs or security; it is the environment, the global carbon footprint. What will be the effect of three to four billion people driving cars and turning on their heating or air conditioners? Is this sustainable?

Jan Willem Blankert[1]

[1] I wrote most of this book in March–June, 2008, during a sabbatical year from the European Commission, as a senior fellow at the Lee Kuan Yew School of Public Policy of the National University of Singapore. The opinions expressed in this book are my own.

Acknowledgements

During the years of dealing with economic and political analysis and reform from Africa, Germany (after reunification) and Poland to the Balkan and China, I have been fortunate in being able to discuss reform policies, on numerous occasions, with many colleagues and friends. I am grateful *to* many analysts and *to* hands-on policy makers who worked with me on these issues and took time to speak to me — and also *to* the participants who discussed with me at the seminars and conferences.

I owe, furthermore, a great debt of gratitude *to* those who have taken their time through years of their lives for their insightful and well-informed articles and books on the subject. In this book, I refer explicitly *to* a number of them, but I am indebted *to* many other authors, not explicitly mentioned, in helping me form and refine my thoughts.

I am also as grateful as every researcher in today's world would *to* the creators of the Internet and Google possibly as significant inventions for mankind as the wheel. These tools, taken together, give all computer-literates immediate access to tremendous wealth of knowledge in a richly endowed library.

Finally I am indebted *to* Klaus Kading and Bertin Martens, for their helpful suggestions on the draft manuscript.

Contents

About This Book: Main Issues

The challenges and opportunities for the West[2] resulting from China's very rapid economic growth are many. The mere size of China makes what one can say about this "China challenge" to a large extent, and *mutatis mutandis*, applicable to India and Asia and globalisation in general. Much has been written about the subject. Have I been able to add something new? Some of this book's added value is no other than linking various views that can be found elsewhere in a more scattered way. I put the narrative, however, more in a European perspective than most of the (American) analysis on the subject offers. I deal with three questions, which are of the greatest interest and which divide this paper in three parts.

First, what is the economist's explanation of a sudden growth spurt like China's (and India's and other Asian countries) today? That is: if there is an explanation. I will review what has been said about **the main determinants of long-term economic growth**. Economic growth as we take it for granted today, with a doubling of living standards practically during each generation, is a relatively young phenomenon. The period from 1750 to now constitutes a unique era in economic history. Today's rich Western countries began to find the path to steady economic progress around 1750. In a sense, China's — and India's and Asia's — growth spurt in the last decades is less surprising than the fact that it took them so long to find this path to greater prosperity. China's growth recipe has worked and delivered so far, but how sustainable is this growth path given the challenges of

---

[2] Used throughout this text in a loose sense and most of the time meaning "the EU and the US" although by implication also Oceania and Canada should be included and where the subject is "rich countries" in fact Japan and Korea too — rich, but geographically obviously not "Western".

income inequality, environmental destruction and corruption? And related to that: does a country *need* democracy once it has achieved a certain wealth level? Like steady economic progress, democracy as we take it for granted today is a relatively young phenomenon. If we assume or hope that economic prosperity eventually will lead to democracy (as citizens who can buy what they want also want to say what they want), countries that are not democratic yet, may become democratic once their standards of living have passed a critical level.

Second, what to make of the debate about **China (India, Asia) unfairly competing and stealing "our" jobs? Are there new insights telling us that globalisation, after being preached by the West for so long, may after all not be as good an idea as we thought and said it was?** Increased capital mobility exposes labour in the West to greater competition from the "reserve army" of labour in low-wage countries. Still, it would seem that over the whole *countries* ahead in the race don't have to suffer from catching-up by others provided these countries continue to be assertive and willing to reform.[3] However, certain *people* and sub-groups in these richer countries may, in particular unskilled labour. This latter development may be at the basis of the observed *decrease* of income inequalities *between* countries (as poor countries are catching up), together with an *increase* of income inequalities *within* countries (as certain segments of the population in rich countries are unable to compete with the newcomers). It would seem that rich Western countries should, nevertheless, welcome Asia's rise and remain open to it; one can only hope that Africa's rise will be next. Trade measures in the form of duties are *not*, as it is presented, imposed on exporting countries or exporting companies, although these countries may suffer from it too. In essence (higher) trade duties are nothing else than a tax on the citizens and business in the importing countries concerned, discouraging competition from abroad and punishing those who prefer foreign products to domestic ones.

---

[3] "Globalisation enriches EU, study says", Financial Times, 29 February, 2008.

Third, the questions raised by Malthus two centuries ago and, subsequently, by the Club of Rome in the 1970s, haunt us once again today. **Will it be possible, to find a sustainable way to live a comfortable life not only with sufficient food, but also with cars and air conditioners when this is no longer the privilege of a happy few, but within reach for four billion people or more?** There are calculations that the annual destruction to China's environment amounts to 5 percent or more of its Gross Domestic Product (GDP). China could soon face a very serious sustainability problem; on an optimistic note, one may point out that countries that are rich today have also gone through such a stage. True, but this time many more people are concerned and hence their lifestyle affects a much larger part of the globe than it was the case before. In addition, much damage has already been done to the environment; is there room for more destruction? This is the challenge of the environment and the availability of resources, which goes way beyond environmental problems in China. The real big question is how we can envisage and accommodate a decent life for all on this planet in a sustainable way. It would imply that by 2050, annual world income — now 65 trillion USD per year, shared by 6.6 billion people — may have to be as high as 300 or 400 trillion USD per year, to be shared by nine billion people who all want to drive cars and eat meat!

Much of the literature on "China and the West" is made in the USA and therefore focuses on the US. At best reference is made to "the West" without giving due attention to the particularities of the EU (the world's largest economy today) or to perceptions on the issue in the EU. In this paper I make an attempt to redress this bias. The point is not without significance. A closer look at the concerns about the China "threat"/job losses, and related calls for greater protectionism as expressed on each side of the Atlantic reveals interesting differences. In the US concerns about the "China threat" usually come from politicians of the Democratic Party and union leaders. To put it simply, China and globalisation are a "left/right" issue. In the EU, on the other hand, it is much more a North/South issue. In Europe, worries about competition from China relate more often to specific cases (such as textiles or shoes from China), and, more significantly, they are expressed by political leaders, but also employers in *Southern* EU Member States. True, in some quarters in the EU there are forceful voices against globalisation and economic integration in all its forms, including integration in Europe.[4] For the moment this concerns, however, groups of limited size at both the utter left and utter right side of the political spectrum where communism and anti-capitalist fascism meet, not mainstream parties or major unions.

Another question I will address is whether the EU, possibly with the exception of some of the Southern EU Member States, may be in a better position than the US to face competition from China (and globalisation in general). To explain the difference a number of factors can be mentioned. First, individual European countries, in particular the smaller ones, have a longer history than the US of exposure to and dependence on foreign trade. Second, Europe's more inclusive and egalitarian society, Europe's "social model" may lead to a greater feeling of security among European workers than exists among their US counterparts. This more inclusive European "model" not only leads to less income inequality, but also, it seems, to less "education inequality" through greater access to education, in particular secondary education, of satisfactory quality. The US is excellent at excelling, but Europe has, it seems, a wider overall distribution of knowledge throughout the population. It may be the case that this enables workers at the lower end of the employment ladder in Europe to adjust more easily to new jobs of acceptable quality.[5]

---

[4] These may include calls for closing the French border for Spanish "imports", as if California were to close its borders for "imports" from other parts of the US.

[5] Income inequality as expressed by the Gini coefficient is 0.31 in the EU, 0.45 in the US. OECD PISA scores (on general knowledge among 15-year olds) are higher in the Northern EU than in the US (and Southern EU).

Chapter I

In Perspective: Long-Term Economic Growth

I.1. Consequences of China's Rise

The flood of books, papers and conferences on the subject of China's rise, and Asia's rise more in general, is hard to cope with. Stark titles and sub-titles seek to seduce would-be-readers. But is the rise of China and let us add India or even "Asia" (or "emerging Asian economies"), really such a new phenomenon? In the 18th and 19th century, beginning with the Netherlands, followed by Britain and most of the rest of Western European countries and the United States found the key to steady economic growth, as we take for granted today and which has allowed for a doubling of living standards in every one or two generations. Today's China hype reminds one of a similar hype surrounding the rise of Japan in the 1980s. Or a French outcry about "Le Défi Americain", published in 1973, according to which corporate Europe would be "eaten up" by American investors.

In a sense it is more surprising that it took so many countries so long to follow after Western economies took off. Whatever the underlying historical explanation for this "delay", it led some observers to believe that stagnation and lasting poverty was the inevitable fate of the majority of Asia and Africa ("coloured people"?). It was even argued that protestant religion and culture made (white?) people better equipped to develop capitalism and build thriving economies. Singapore's Kishore Mahbubani touches at it in his "Can Asians think?".[6] In spite of this catchy title, the issue he really addresses in

---

[6] Kishore Mahbubani, Can Asians Think?, 2004.

1

the essay from which his book derives its title is not if Asians can think, but if they can achieve the same level of welfare as the West. His answer is a clear "yes".

And we are getting that same answer every day now from Asia: yes, Asians can "think", or rather: Asians are very well able to improve their living standards. And why would they not? Until 1750/1800, before the West set of to an economic growth spurt that would last until today, China and India between them accounted for some 50 percent of world GDP. Subsequently, China, which had very much closed its economy from foreign trade and culture, saw *relative* decline against the background of the technology driven productivity growth and rising income levels in the West. This didn't improve after the West, in 1842, forced China to open up and participate in the international trade game as dictated by the West. At that same time, India's economy grew by an estimated 0.5 percent per year, until 1948.

Japan had already in the 19th century found the "key to growth" and modernisation. In the 1950's and the 1960's the Asian tigers, Hong Kong, Korea, Singapore and Taiwan followed. China first went through its devastating "Great Leap Forward" and the chaos of the Cultural Revolution, but in 1978 it, finally, found the key too, followed by India in 1991. I use the word "key", because the study of economic development makes economic growth almost look like a door that can be opened, a light that can be switched on. Put the right policies in place and off you go. Telling is the story of Chinese leader Deng Xiaoping who, in 1978, visited Thailand, Malaysia, Korea and Singapore to see "how they did it". Back in China, he just switched China's growth machine on, as it were. Deng turned the page and set China on a path of uninterrupted growth for the next three decades, lasting until today.

Before looking into greater detail at the rise of China and its consequences for the West four remarks are in place. First, as I said, I believe that China's rise (apart from its size, a point which is hard to neglect) is no different from the rise of dozens of countries whose economic rise started centuries or decades before — or at least less different than many want us to believe. Second, in spite of their strong growth performance in the last decades and in spite of great improvements made, both China and India are still very poor countries today with hundreds of millions in deep poverty. China's average standard of living is some 20 percent of living standards in the EU, India's no more than 10 percent. There is great income inequality in both countries. Third, the one factor that makes the rise of China and India so special is the sheer size of their populations, 1.3 billion and 1.1 billion respectively. China and India account between them for 36 percent of the world population. If one adds up the 500 million living in the ASEAN countries,[7] part of which are also catching up very rapidly, the number becomes 2.9 billion, 44 percent of the world population today. Hence their rise inevitably has a huge impact, also for the rest of the world population. Fourth, this latter aspect, population size, becomes particularly telling and of an impact when one thinks of the consequences for the environment and the pressure on scarce resources.

When at New Delhi's Auto Show, in January 2008, the Nano was presented — India's T-Ford or Volkswagen Beetle — with a price tag of USD 2,500, the world watched in awe, but not without concern. What if millions of Indians start driving this cheap car, how about the impact on the environment? The same can be said for the aspirations of China's 1.3 billion. What if China's 1.3 billion will all have electricity, will be able to buy fridges and dishwashers, drive cars and eat more meat? China's car park is growing by 5 million per year and that growth will accelerate, every year. Already today we can feel what China's growth means for the environment and prices of oil, copper, steel and other resources.

The race for bio-fuels and the competition over carbon hydrates between people's stomachs and their cars have added another aspect to the calculus which has helped set food prices on a steady rise. Unless adjustment takes place, policy measures are taken and new technologies developed the pressure can only increase. We are probably only seeing the beginning of this new environmental challenge and renewed competition for alternative uses of resources. Trade and investment questions will pale in comparison as they will pass

---

[7] ASEAN was established in 1967; Member States today are Brunei, Cambodia, Indonesia, Philippines, Laos, Malaysia, Burma/Myanmar, Singapore, Thailand and Vietnam.

Share in world Gross Domestic Product (GDP), at 1990 international USD and average GDP per head

	China	India	Asia (excl. Japan)	Western Europe	USA
Share and per head, 1820	32.9% 600	16.0% 530	56.2% 575	23.6% 1230	1.8% 1260
Share and per head, 1913	8.9% 550	7.6% 670	21.9% 640	33.5% 3470	19.6% 5300
Share and per head, 1950	4.5% 440	4.2% 620	15.5% 635	26.3% 4590	27.3% 9560
Share and per head, 1998	11.5% 3120	5.0% 1750	29.5% 2940	20.6% 17,900	21.9% 27,300

Source: Maddison, The World Economic Millennial Perspective.

in the same way as the Japan hype of the 1980's has blown over. Who is worried about competition from Japan today? Japan has smoothly integrated into the international economy and among others enabled us to drive its excellent, environmentally relatively friendly cars.

I.2. Asia: Finally Getting There?

The debate around the rise of China — and along with it India and other emerging economies in Asia — is overly excited, reminiscent of the exaggerated assessments when Japan was growing at break-speed 25 years ago. A common notion is also the suggestion or prediction of a decline of the West and the disappearance of jobs in the West. Apparently many in the debate have hardly bothered to take time to reflect on or look at similar examples of sudden bursts of economic growth in the past.

The economic rise of the United States in the second half of the 19th century and its continuation in the 20th century have led to a significant change in the balance of power in the world; that is worth to reflect on. But, for instance, the standard of living of British citizens and British national income, and also that of other nations, while becoming *relatively* less important, has only increased and is still increasing. In spite of and possibly precisely because of America's economic rise people in Britain were better of in 1875 and in 1900 than they had been before and since then their living standards have, once again, improved tremendously. The increased economic power of the newcomers should of course be reflected in their representation in international bodies. The existence of the so-called G-8 in its present form (including Canada and Italy as members, but without China) is an anomaly which should be corrected.

At the time I write this, in early 2008, both EU and US policy makers lament about the bilateral trade deficits they have with China. But the EU, in spite of its bilateral trade deficit with China of 250 billion euros in 2007 has a positive trade balance and a balanced current account balance with the world as a whole. The deficit with China is compensated by surpluses with other trading partners. In the first half of 2008, unemployment in the EU was at a 25-year low. Could it be that cheap inputs from China keep the EU economy ticking and that the EU has little to worry about?

Let me reiterate that one particular aspect makes the rise of China and India special: the sheer size of these countries in terms of population. China and India together have a population of 2.4 billion, 36 percent of the world population of 6.6 billion. The EU and the US together account for 800 million people, 12 percent of the world population. The rich economies together, account for some 15 percent of the world population. At the same time, in spite of rapid economic growth in China and India and in spite of the fact that hundreds of millions have been lifted out of dire poverty, many of their people are still poor: hundreds of millions in these countries still live in poverty. In other words: more and continuous growth is still needed in these countries.

Is there really reason to worry and lament for the West about the "competitive threat" when we see how these countries, first, may in fact contribute to our wealth (see the reference in Footnote 3 on page x) and, second, finally have found out how to climb up the ladder and reach living standards somewhat closer to, albeit still much lower than those in the West? Once again, a more interesting question is why it took these countries so long to find the key to greater prosperity. Is there something mysterious in why and how economies grow?

I.3. China's Rise in Perspective

It may be useful to remember how relatively young the phenomenon of economic growth as we know it and have got accustomed to is — i.e., the steady, significant annual rise of economic productivity and output per worker, only interrupted by brief periods of recession. That pattern, that we are now so used if not addicted to, has existed for only a little more than two centuries. Until the second half of the 18th century slow economic progress with an annual growth of no more than half a percent per year, was the norm, just enough (or not enough) to keep up with population growth. It brought Thomas Robert Malthus (1766–1834) to his theory that economic growth would never be able to keep up with population growth and that therefore in the long run impoverishment and famine would be inevitable.

According to data constructed, over many years and from many sources, by Angus Maddison — the guru of long-term economic development — up until somewhere around the year 1800 the economies of China and India combined accounted, for many centuries, for close to 50 percent of world gross domestic product (GDP). Today their combined share of the world's annual economic output is somewhere between 15 percent and 20 percent, the best guess is 17 percent. But that is after three decades of very high growth in China and sixteen years of accelerated growth in India; after a long "recovery" of these two giants from the time, in 1950, that they accounted jointly for no more than a meagre 9 percent of the world's GDP.

This declining *share* is mostly explained by the rapid *rise* — economic growth — in other parts of the world, not by an *absolute decline* in China or India. In a long term perspective all areas of the world have seen some economic growth in the last two centuries. But, for instance, during the period 1820 to 1952 the Chinese economy grew by a mere 0.2 percent per year, less than the rate of population growth.

During that same period annual economic growth in the US was 3.8 percent, in "Europe" and Japan 1.7 percent and in Russia 2 percent. So whereas China and India stagnated in the period between 1800 and 1950 other parts of the world saw a rapid growth rally. What we see today is therefore not more than *China and India finally catching up.*

Against the backdrop of the rapid economic expansion in the US, Europe, Japan and the Soviet Union/Russia after 1800, China and India seemed, until 30 or 25 years ago, lost cases in economic terms. Since then, first, China has seen very rapid economic growth. And now also India is reporting growth rates nearing 10 percent per year. In a way these two countries are emerging after a long-term slump. Probably it is today's best economic news. Thanks to China's phenomenal growth of the last two decades, millions have been lifted out of poverty. The estimates are between 400 million for China and 300 million for India, more than could have been achieved with any aid programme, whatever its scale.

Until a few years ago there was suspicion that China inflated its growth figures for propaganda reasons, that growth was in fact lower than reported. Gradually Western observers started to believe the Chinese figures. In 2005, the results of a business census led to China to revise its GDP upwards by as much as 17 percent. Chinese statisticians literally "discovered" a vast amount of economic activity that had been going on without statisticians noticing it. The main reason was that China's communist past made its statistical system better equipped to measure "hardware", tons of steel and butter produced, than "software", mostly activities taking place in the services sector, such as economic output in the form of haircuts, retail activity or tourism.

However, in spite of this high growth and all the hype *China is still a poor country.* Per capita income in purchasing power parities (PPP)[8] — i.e., what one can buy for one's money, the "standard of

---

[8] PPP = not using exchange rates only, but also taking into account differences in price levels between countries, accounting for the fact that 100 euros buys more eggs or shoes say in China than in the EU.

living" — is at best 20 percent of the EU average and by consequence some 14 percent of the US average. Living standards in India are on average something like 10 percent of those in the EU, 7 percent when compared with the US (and possibly lower). Rapid economic growth in China has led to calculations predicting — or speculating — when the Chinese economy may be "overtaking" the US economy. Some put this event at 2025. Extrapolating today's growth rates suggests that the Chinese economy could "bypass" the US economy somewhere around 2040 and much earlier even if we take purchasing power parities as the basis of our calculation.

But what does "bypassing" or "overtaking" mean? Today there are 1.3 billion Chinese and 300 million Americans. If we assume, on the basis of population growth rates, that there will be three times as many Chinese as Americans in 2040, "overtaking" would only mean that, *on average*, the Chinese would have reached a level of welfare *one third* that of a US citizen (by then). By the same token (and at present trends), China's average welfare level might be somewhere around half — with a little luck more — that of the EU. On the scale of EU today's standards of living "ladder" China might be somewhere where Poland is today (67 percent of the average of the EU of 27). We can only hope for better living standards for the people of China and India — and for ourselves.

Has the rise of the US and American prosperity in the 19th and 20th century been a threat to Europe? The answer that makes most sense in economic terms is: no, probably not, probably to the contrary. One can say the same for Japan's rise. And the same will apply, once again, for the rise of China and India. The "recovery" of China and India should not make us believe that their gain is our loss. Has the West not told dozens of poor countries, time and again, that globalization, international trade and competition are a win-win game?

The West can only hope that China and India will manage to reach one day — still decades away — average levels of prosperity that today the majority of EU citizens take for granted. That would be good for them, but also for us. It will mean that the EU's relative share in world GDP will shrink. But the issue, the challenge for the

EU is: levels of productivity and GDP within the EU. The challenge for Europe (and the US) will be to get its own economic act together, which means that Europe and the US should further improve education, research and development and infrastructure to maintain steady productivity growth and ensure continued growth of their economies.

The time of writing is early 2008 and the world, or economists of the world at least, look in awe at China's economic growth figure for 2007: 11.4 percent. In spite of increasing concern about decline in the US, China's GDP is expected to grow by another 10 percent — 9 percent at least — in 2008. True, rising inflation (5 percent in 2007 and rising to 10 percent at least in 2008) is a concern. How about India? Not exactly the same, but also there has been very high growth, most probably once again something like of 8.5 percent and 7 percent at "worst".

As said, the US economy was expected to slow in the course of 2008 and seemed to be sliding into recession, which was to affect the economies of China and India and of other countries too. In particular China, with 20 percent of its exports going to the US saw slower growth. But then, yes, the economists tell us, slower growth in the US may shave off 1 percentage point, perhaps even 1.5 from growth in these two countries in 2008, which would imply that these two growth machines would end up with say a "meagre" 9 percent or 8 percent growth of their economies in 2008, which is still spectacular. Supposing that this assessment will prove to be correct, this would form demonstration of the strength of these economies.

I.4. Long-Term Growth: Where Does It Come From?

The most intriguing question remains where this economic growth comes from. The simple, but not very helpful answer, is given by Mancur Olson in an article in Economic Perspectives. In short, it is "sound economic policy":

> Since neither differences in endowments of any of the three classical aggregate factors of production nor differential access to technology

Basic comparative data, 2007 (unless indicated otherwise)

	China	EU	India	USA	World
Population in bln. (in brackets % of world pop.)	1.3 (20%)	0.5 (7.5%)	1.1 (17%)	0.3 (4.5%)	6.7 (100%)
Infant mortality per 1000 live births	21	6.4	32	6.3	42.0
Life expectancy at birth	73	77	69	78	66
GDP (PPP, see footnote 6) trln USD	8.0 (12%)	14.4 (22%)	3.0 (5%)	13.9 (21%)	65.8 (100%)
GDP, PPP/per head, USD; in brackets: % of world average	6,150 (61%)	33,000 (330%)	2,700 (27%)	46,000 (460%)	10,000 (100%)
GDP at exchange rate, trln. USD	2.9	16.6	1.1	13.8	54.6
Income distr. (Gini)[9]	47	30	37	45	
Exports, % GDP	42%	9%	16%	8.2%	25%
Exports, trln. USD % world exports	1.2 (8.6%)	1.3 (9.4%)	0.15 (1.0%)	1.14 (8.1%)	13.9 (100%)
Electricity production, trillion KWh	3.2	3.0	0.67	4.0	18.6
Electricity production/ head, KWh	2,500	6,000	610	13,300	2,770
Cell phones per 1000 population	385	950	150	785	310
Internet users per 1000 population	125	500	54	690	150
Automobiles, mln	30	230	12	240	
Automobiles/1000	23	460	11	800	
Military expenditure, % GDP	4.3%	2.0%	2.5%	4.5%	2.0%
CO_2 emissions, 2004, (million metric tons and % of world total	5,000 (17%)	4,000 (14%)	1,300 (4.5%)	6,200 (21%)	29,000 (100%)
CO_2 emissions, 2004, tonnes per capita	3.8	8.1	1.2	20.6	4.4

Source: CIA World Factbook with some own estimates.
trln: trillion; mln: million.

---

[9] Zero means there is no income inequality: everybody receives the same; 100 = 100 percent inequality: one gets all.

explain much of the great variation in per capita incomes, we are left with the second of the two (admittedly highly aggregated) possibilities set out above: that much the most important explanation of the differences in income across countries is the difference in their economic policies and institutions.[10]

Olson leaves us empty-handed as he doesn't give us an insight as to which economic policies to follow with his tautological "advice". Elmahan Helpman is more explicit by listing elements that an economic policy for growth should contain. In order to achieve economic growth, Helpman argues, a country needs *productivity growth* — but that is rather a statement of the obvious. Admittedly, he elaborates on the drivers of this productivity growth: innovation fed by research and development, subsequently the accumulation and diffusion of knowledge, trade and other exchanges (e.g., of technology) and, finally, again the less tangible factor "institutions and politics" although the latter are specified by the key expressions property rights, rule of law, limits on the power of rulers.[11]

In her "The Elephant and the Dragon" Robyn Meredith describes how, in 1978, Chinese leader Deng Xiaoping, aware that China had to modernise, visited Bangkok, Kuala Lumpur, Seoul and Singapore to see how modernisation worked. Meredith says the following about Deng's meetings with Singapore's Lee Kuan Yew:

The two men held three days of talks, and as Deng toured Singapore, he found a modern, technologically advanced nation suitable as a model for China's development. "That journey was an eye-opener for him," said Mr. Lee decades later, "a turning point". It was indeed, both for Deng and for China. The ethnically Chinese city-state of Singapore was, and remains, famous worldwide for its stable, one-party rule and its lack of freedoms (…) as well as its remarkably rapid transformation from a developing country to a modern, capitalist one. The government heavily planned Singapore's economic development, building modern

[10] Mancur Olson Jr., "Why Some Nations are Rich, and Others Poor", in The Journal of Economic Perspectives, Spring, 1996.
[11] Elhanan Helpman, The Mystery of Economic Growth, 2004.

infrastructure and attracting foreign investment. Pro-business policies made the city an export powerhouse and quickly raised the standard of living of its people. China's attitude adjustment was radical and immediate.

The quote once again suggests that the key to economic development is just there to grab and open the door.[12] The path is not necessarily the same for all countries and there is no standard policy recipe. China certainly did not follow the standard recipe recommended at the time, which was to move quickly. It chose a gradual approach, no sudden shock, and decided to give economic reform priority and leave political reform out of the equation. But both China and India put great effort at improving education, putting research and development high on their agenda, introducing principles of market economics and, possibly a more mundane purely economic criterion, both ensured sound fiscal and monetary policies. So in a way the changes beginning with China in 1978, after the country's bankruptcy following the Cultural Revolution, and in India, after hesitation, but under the pressure of untenable external financial constraints, boils down to the political leadership "simply" turning the page and deciding (choosing) for a new policy.

I.5. Seven Pillars of Western Wisdom and the Soft Infrastructure of Capitalism

Kishore Mahbubani, reviewing the growth drivers in the particular case of Asia, defines what he refers to as the "seven pillars of Western wisdom": "The Japanese learned well: they found — as the four tigers found a century later, and China and India have realized during the past two decades — that there were at least seven pillars of Western wisdom that could have an almost *miraculous* (emphasis mine) effect on their societies." Those seven pillars are, according to Mahbubani: 1) free

---

[12] Henri Ghesquiere in "Singapore's Success" (2007) refers to it as "the seemingly secret key to unlocking the potential"; the subtitle of his book is, very appropriately, "*Engineering* economic growth" (emphasis mine).

market economics; 2) science and technology; 3) meritocracy; 4) pragmatism; 5) culture of peace; 6) rule of law and 7) education.[13]

One may wonder whether the inclusion of the "culture of peace" in this equation, welcome as it may be, can be justified. Does this not overlook the fact that Europe has seen devastating wars in the last century, which although interrupting its long-term growth spurt have not halted it? We may of course take a shorter term view and consider Europe's change of mood and mind with the creation of the European Union and the EU's "soft power" and active support to multilateral institutions in the second half of the 20th century as more characteristic than this previous experience.

Still, speaking about "the West" there remains a big question mark over this "peace pillar" when one considers the export of violence by the US. One doesn't have to be a fan of Naomi Klein and believe in the distorted picture she presents of a US conspiracy in the name of Milton Friedman in practically everything the US has been doing abroad in the last decades,[14] to acknowledge that there has been a considerable amount of exported violent action and warfare by the US.

The US figures number 97 on the "Global Peace Index" and between 1989 and 2001, the United States intervened with force in foreign lands more frequently than at any other time in its history — an average of one significant new military action every sixteen months — and far more than any other power in the same stretch of time. This expansive, even aggressive, global policy was consistent with American foreign policy traditions."[15] There may be a wish and a theory of preaching peace, but how credible is that when practice is so different? One may easily argue that at present the US is the most aggressive nation on the globe.

How about democracy? Is democracy not a pre-condition for steady economic growth? Do we not at least hope or believe it is?

---

[13] Kishore Mahbubani, The New Asian Hemisphere, 2008.
[14] Naomi Klein, The Shock Doctrine, 2007.
[15] Robert Kagan, The Return of History and the End of Dreams, 2008.

According to UNDP data, among the 25 richest economies in the world in 2007,[16] 23 can be qualified as open democratic societies (to be noted: Italy, which I count among the democracies, is by the Economist Intelligence Unit (EIU) ranked as a "flawed democracy").[17] The two small city economies of Singapore and Hong Kong, which complete the 25, may be seen as "special cases". Among the next 25 on the list of richest nations, the numbers 26 to 50, there are no more than seven democracies, 14 "flawed democracies" and four "authoritarian regimes". Of the 25 poorest nations of the world according to UNDP 15 are listed as "authoritarian regimes by the EIU, 8 as "hybrid regimes" and a meagre two as "flawed democracies". So there seems to be some relationship at least between prosperity and democracy, but the question is: how does that relationship work? Does democracy come with (as a result of) prosperity or does a country need democracy to grow — or, more accurately, to *be* rich?

Democracy may come in many forms and shapes and democracy as the West considers as normal and the norm today and as the EU and the US seek to promote or "export" is a relatively new phenomenon — as is the rule of law. When it comes to the question of democracy and China it should be acknowledged that China's citizens enjoy much greater freedom today than they did two decades ago, but China is not a democratic state or a "free democracy". Its own leaders recognise that. But then, again, is democracy not a pre-condition for growth, as many in the West think or wish to think? Peter Nolan thinks it is not; comparing transformation in China and Russia he writes:

> Hardly a single country has grown from low to high income in a democratic framework. Contrary to popular belief, none of the advanced economies had mass democracy in the early stage of modern economic growth. During the take-off phase virtually all of them were governed by liberal principles which granted political rights to

---

[16] GDP/PPP data in UNDP: "Human Development Report, 2007/2008", on http://hdrstats.undp.org/indicators.

[17] www.economist.com/media/pdf/DEMOCRACY_TABLE_2007_v3.pdf

property holders, but did not mostly allow political power to be granted to the urban or rural proletariat, to impoverished racial minorities or women. The development of mass democracy *followed* (emphasis mine) rather than preceded the take-off. This has been the case too in successful industrializers in the late twentieth century.[18]

So, on this account and it seems difficult to refute it entirely, democracy should rather be seen as the *product* of growth, the *consequence* of greater prosperity. Another sobering reminder that democracy is a relatively new phenomenon comes from Larry Diamond of the Hoover Institution: "In 1900 there was not a single country in the world that would qualify as a democracy by today's standards. As of January 2000, there were 120 democracies, the highest number in the history of the world".[19]

Perhaps it makes sense to qualify "democracy" and to use Will Hutton's expression "the soft infrastructure of capitalism", a notion he extensively elaborates on in his "The Writing on the Wall".[20] Elements of Hutton's "soft infrastructure" are, for instance, civil society — from religious organisations to Green Peace and from School Parents Committees to labour unions and consumer organisations, but one may also think of professional guilds for instance in 18th century Europe, media including critical media, books (Dickens, Marx, Engels), property rights and a properly functioning judiciary.

Hutton sees these "institutions", developed during enlightenment, part of them well *before* political democratisation, all as an important, if not indispensable factor, counterbalance and corrective mechanism to market forces. Civil society organisations and media have been indispensable in drawing the attention to poverty and health hazards in what are rich democracies today, enabling corrective action already before there were electoral democracies in place. Some of these factors — as said: part of the tissue of society before full

---

[18] Peter Nolan, Transforming China, 2004.

[19] Larry Diamond, A Report Card on Democracy, Hoover Institution, www.hoover.org/publications/digest.

[20] Will Hutton, *The Writing on the Wall*, 2006.

democratisation — are not present in today's China. So will China be able to generate necessary corrective action where needed?

Income disparities and environmental destruction are among the most serious of China's growth pains. China's political leaders are aware and seek to reduce and correct these pains. It remains to be seen, however, whether China's top-down approach with which it seeks to remedy these pains is sufficient without Hutton's "soft infrastructure" providing feedback and counterbalance. China may have learned important lessons from Singapore and have prospered on the basis of those lessons, but Singapore's population of 4.3 million may make it a special case (like the small European growth "tigers" Ireland, Estonia and Luxembourg are cases of their own).

It may be easier to govern small-scale Singapore in semi-authoritarian style, as a family as it were, than China, the most populous state on earth. For Singapore's rulers it may be possible to receive direct feedback from its 4.3 million people, living on 630 square kilometres, and apply appropriate corrective measures. *Mutatis mutandis*, for China's rulers, who are in charge of a country of 1.3 billion on 10 million square kilometres, this may be a much more complicated matter. This leads in the case of China to the question not whether *greater* democracy, or soft infrastructure of capitalism, is *desirable*, but whether it may be *required* to make China's economic growth sustainable. On the basis of the experience of rich nations (see quote from Nolan above) one may reason that it is open to question at which income level democracy (or greater democracy?) is needed. And perhaps sustainable growth can be achieved by the *gradual* introduction of democratic principles (as it was in fact the case in many Western countries).

One may also consider China's reform process versus India's. In the case of India it is often claimed that as India is a democracy, it can be more complicated to implement reforms there than in China. Ironically, there are examples where India's Communists blocked the government from implementing reforms the Communist regime in Beijing was able to go ahead with unhindered. Nolan reminds us of the scepticism that existed among both Western economists and within China's Communist Party itself with regard to China's reforms. It was argued that democracy and privatisation were pre-conditions for long-term economic growth whereas in China the party remained firm in control:

> The fact that the Chinese system of political economy in the 1980s was "market socialist" and yet was one of the most dynamic in terms both of output and income growth that the modern world had seen, presents economists with a puzzle: why did it perform so well in the first decade and a half of reform, despite the fact that the economic institutions were gravely inadequate in relation to mainstream Western economic theory and policy? (...) A more worrying possibility is that China's incrementalist approach to economic reform may have been correct and the attempt in most of Eastern Europe and in the former USSR to move rapidly towards a market economy may have been a serious mistake.[21]

Nolan suggests that there may have been a "huge inherent catch-up and overtaking possibility which may have been latent in all former Stalinist economies on account of the vast under-performance in relation to their huge physical and human capital inheritance." In reply to this it can be pointed out that the former Soviet Republics in East Asia, who haven't followed a standard textbook quick-fix solution either, are still poor and non-democratic today whereas the East European former Satellites, in particular Poland, have gone the whole way from rapid "shock therapy" and impoverishment initially to normalcy today, including improved and further improving living standards and democratic regimes.

Poland and other former communist states that have joined the European Union in the meantime have returned to "normalcy" relatively quickly. These countries turned into democracies at an early stage of the transformation process and later in the process their economies started growing again, admittedly, all of them after initially seeing large falls in output. The prospect of joining the EU influenced

---

[21] Peter Nolan, *Transforming China*, 2004.

the transformation process and not least the predictability of the transformation and hence how economic prospects were perceived, among others by investors, including foreign ones.

What can be said in the case of China is that in spite of China's impressive growth performance so far, it remains to be seen whether China once it reaches middle-income status will be able to maintain today's balance of the "socialist market economy" with its firm one-party rule. As I pointed out, the question is raised within the Chinese Communist Party (CCP) itself. Recently it was addressed in a report by the Party School in which it is argued that greater freedom is indispensable for the Party to maintain its legitimacy and stay in power.[22]

I.6. Democracy and Indicators of Good Governance

The West strongly feels that (greater) democracy in China is desirable. The EU has active dialogue with China ongoing on human rights. One of the very modest wishes on the EU list is that China finally ratifies the UN Covenant on Civil and Political Rights (UNCCPR), which it signed in 1997, but so far China is holding off. The EU urges China to revise its penitential system and its approach to the death penalty. Both the EU and the US plead for the freeing of specific prisoners, not least those involved with the Tiananmen incident in 1989 who are still detained. The advent of the Olympic Games in Beijing in the summer of 2008, is leading to increased scrutiny of China's human rights situation by international media and the public alike. China is not impressed, but expectations are rising and tension is increasing. In March 2008, the situation in Tibet exploded, spreading to neighbouring Sichuan. Could there be more unrest, in other areas too? The Chinese authorities do not make an effort to pretend that China is a democratic state in the Western

---

[22] "Storming the Fortress: A research report on China's political system reform after the 17th party congress", in the *Financial Times*, 20 February, 2008:... "leading scholars have recognised the need for formal checks on the party's power, both through a strengthened legal system and freer media".

sense. They stress the very considerable improvements in the rights of China's population over the last decades, which are undeniable, and make two further points.

First, the Chinese leadership does not have the intention to introduce Western style democracy in China. Second, yes, there will be greater freedom for Chinese citizens, but only once the climate is ripe. This debate is, again, about the *wish* (above all, of the West) to have (greater) democracy in China. As we saw, within China's Communist Party discussion is ongoing about the possible *need* to introduce greater democracy. This less for reasons of principle than of pragmatism and on the basis of the assumption that some time somehow China's citizens will want to have a greater say.

The Chinese leadership has started releasing figures of demonstrations and riots that take place. In general and leaving aside Tibet, these demonstrations are typically triggered by corruption by local officials, cases of excessive pollution or the infringement of property rights or the right to continue to *use* land or housing. In particular the latter can be seen as "a test of the potential for political activism among the new middle class, especially residents of the wealthier cities who have acquired their own property" and "These protests suggest there could be limits on government ability to pursue big projects in urban areas".[23] Construction works for the Olympic Games have led to many evictions, leading to protests. The CCP is aware of the risks involved and thinking of ways to channel public anger — think of Hutton's "soft infrastructure of capitalism".

The question whether countries *need* democracy to *grow* is in a general, academic way dealt with by Przeworski and Limongi (P&L) in their little jewel "Political Regimes and Economic Growth".[24] I term it a jewel because the authors so clearly refuse to take any "conventional wisdom" for granted. They begin by pointing out that "while everyone seems to agree that secure property rights foster growth, it is controversial whether democracies or dictatorships better

---

[23] "Friction suspends work on Shanghai maglev", *Financial Times*, 7 March, 2008.
[24] Adam Przeworski and Fernando Limongi, "Political Regimes and Economic Growth", in *Journal of Economic Perspectives*, Number 3, 1993.

secure these rights" and continue with "*The idea that democracy protects property rights is a recent invention, and we think a far-fetched one.*" (emphasis mine). P&L remind the reader that the economic consequences of democracy were at the centre of debates concerning the rights to vote and to organise during the first half of the nineteenth century. Conservatives and socialists — as for the latter, including Karl Marx — agreed that "democracy, specifically universal suffrage and the freedom to form unions, must threaten property." The authors have bothered to compare 18 studies on the subject by other researchers, resulting in the comparison of 21 samples of countries during certain periods. P&L draw the following sobering conclusion from this:

> Among them (note: these 21 findings), eight found in favour of democracy, eight in favour of authoritarianism, and five discovered no difference. What is even more puzzling is that among the 11 results published before 1988, eight found that authoritarian regimes grew faster, while none of the nine results published after 1987 supported this finding. And since this difference does not seem attributable to samples or periods, one can only wonder about the relations between statistics and ideology. For reasons discussed below we hesitate to attach much significance to these results one way or another. Hence, we still do not know what the facts are.

To be fair to the studies that are compared, P&L do not mention the possibility that the more favourable outcome for democracy in more recent research could be related to the fact that, as I found, the more recent studies span periods which, unlike what P&L state about sample periods, on average end in 1988, whereas those where the conclusion is that authoritarian regimes are better for growth end on average in 1980, i.e., earlier. So the more favourable outcome for democracy *may* be the reflection of the fact that democracy has been (or was) "on the winning hand" rather than of researchers' "ideology" (as P&L suggest).

It is a sobering conclusion nevertheless, for a reader in 2008, almost two decades after the collapse of the Soviet Union and the fall of communism in Eastern Europe and after a period of a triumphant mood in the West about "the victory of capitalism", which led even to a short-sighted, infantile and short-lived belief in "the end of history". Today, many may have forgotten (even never heard of) the shock and concern the launch of the Sputnik by the Soviet Union in 1957 caused in the West. The fear was that the West might be "overtaken by the Soviets". Today's Western reader may indeed take both democracy and its supposed positive effect on economic growth too easily for granted.

We should, however, not forget that the P&L study is about democracy and economic *growth*, not the *level* of income achieved. There remains the fact that the 25 richest economies of the world today are predominantly democracies and none of the 25 poorest are. So, again, should democracy then perhaps be seen as the *product* of growth rather, the *consequence* of greater prosperity? Can one imagine today a rich country with a well-to-do middle-class, which is not at the same time a fully-fletched competitive, electoral democracy with free-speech? Singapore is perhaps the one and only example one can come up with.

William Easterly produces a table showing how democracy increases with income (or the other way round, the causality is not clarified). A bar chart for four groups of countries is shown: from "quarter least democratic" to "quarter most democratic, with average income levels (in 2002) represented as bars, gradually rising from 1,000 USD on average in the first group to 15,000 in the fourth. Easterly provides, however, no further explanation or the basis of his selection of countries and calculations.[25]

A graph on the subject in Henri Ghesquiere's (HG) "Singapore's Success" is more transparent. HG, ranks countries by their degree of democracy (according to "Freedom House") on a scale of 1 (low) to 7 (high) on the horizontal axis and plots their GDP/PPP on the vertical axis. His graph shows, first, that the statistical relationship is a weak one at best; and, second, that only countries scoring a 7 (highest) for

---

[25] William Easterly, *The White Man's Burden: Why the West's Efforts to Aid the Rest Have Done So Much Ill and So Little Good*, 2006; page 130.

democracy are on average in a clearly higher income group than the rest. But then again, as HG points out "the direction of the causation is not self-evident".[26] So do we have an answer now to the question whether China *needs* democracy to continue growing? No, we don't. At best we may conclude that as China climbs the economic ladder the chances for greater democracy will improve.

Today's wisdom is that *institutions* are crucial for ensuring growth. With the valuable and highly interesting World Bank governance indicators countries are given scores on six criteria 1) regulatory quality; 2) government effectiveness; 3) rule of law; 4) control of corruption; 5) voice and accountability (say, "democracy") and 6) stability. In a chapter in *Dancing with Giants*[27] Philip Keefer seeks to match China's and India's impressive growth performance with these criteria. It appears, however, that both China and India score not more than average on these governance indicators. India, not surprisingly, scores higher than China on "voice and accountability whereas China does better on "government effectiveness", also not a surprise. So how to explain that China and India combine impressive growth performance with such mediocre governance scores? Keefer, rightly pointing out that this is a "puzzle", first argues that China's and India's scores although modest are still better than those of poorer countries. It is a good reminder once again, that on any measure and in spite of their strong growth both China and India still are poor countries on average.

In his further effort to understand and explain the "puzzle" Keefer introduces market size as an *additional* explanatory factor. That market size matters or may matter has often been argued and would be difficult to deny. Market size can help manufacturers to build up capacity and create economies of scale in the home market before starting to explore export markets. The argument has been used for explaining America's growth and prosperity, arguably the clearest example.

---

[26] Henri Guesquiere, Singapore's Success, 2007, page 158. On more than once occasion the author points at Singapore's position as a "statistical outlier", an exception to the rule.

[27] Philip Keefer, "Governance and Economic Growth", in *Dancing with Giants*, editors L. Alan Winters, Shahid Yusuf, World Bank, 2007.

The market size argument has been used in Europe, to stress the importance of integration into one large market. It was the key argument for Europe's "1992" internal market exercise.

And there is abundant evidence that the size of China's domestic market has been a factor in attracting foreign capital. However, true and valid as the "market size" argument may be, it was not part of the initial equation, i.e., the "good governance explains it all" paradigm. Furthermore, China and India were already large markets long before they started growing rapidly in 1978 and 1991 respectively. The answer to this might be: yes, but governance changes brought about in 1978 in China and in 1991 in India fell on fertile ground there with great potential. But then, when the size of the home market is brought in as a factor, how to explain the successes of, say, tiny Singapore, Ireland, Luxembourg, Estonia and other small, fast growers? The charm of the good governance indicators was that they seemed to be able to explain it all, but the economic profession is a tricky business.

Dani Rodrik and others conclude in a paper that thoroughly examines the factors that determine growth, including geography and the governance indicators: "the distinction between institutions and policy is murky, as these examples illustrate" and "How much guidance do our results provide to policymakers who want to improve the performance of their economies? Not much at all. Sure, it is helpful to know that geography is not destiny, or that focusing on increasing the economy's links with world markets is unlikely to yield convergence. *But the operational guidance that our central result on the primacy of institutional quality yields is extremely meagre* (emphasis mine)."[28] It is also confusing, if not ironic, that whereas property rights and the rule of law are considered as crucial in the context of "institutions", in today's fast growing China the first one of these two is not always assured and the quality of the second is dubious. Also Keefer in his contribution on governance in *Dancing with Giants* has to sort of

---

[28] Dani Rodrik, Arvind Subramanian, Francesco Trebbi: "Institutions Rule: The Primacy of Institutions over Geography and Integration in Economic Development", NBER Working Paper, 2002.

reason away China's actual institutional situation, including democracy (voice and accountability), and explain its growth success (see also the scatter diagrams at the end of this book, which give a "mixed message").

One factor is almost surprisingly absent in most of the more recent analysis, that is direct government intervention in the economy, *the visible hand of government* or active "industrial policy". The term and the subject appear to be no longer fashionable in today's economic analysis. However, it cannot be denied that government played an active role in the growth stories of, for instance, Japan, Korea, Singapore and Taiwan, and earlier on in European countries. With some flexibility China's special zones and the US's high import tariffs in the early stage of the latter's industrialisation process may still be considered as being part of "government regulation". But the role of state-owned industries, including banks, in China today, or in France and Germany early in their industrialisation process, probably deserves greater attention and more thorough analysis than it is the case in most development or growth analysis today (unless one would smuggle them into "institutions", but that is not how I interpret the "institutions are all" scholars).

So have we learned something or is the sobering answer: *growth happens and nobody knows exactly why?* To some extent it is the latter, although many plausible conjectures can be made and factors helping growth indicated. The search for the "key to growth" leads to "indicators", but also to the conclusion that there is not a one-serves-all recipe. Let us also keep in mind that the good governance indicators are all based on subjective assessments made by a multitude of people and organisations. They are as good as they are, i.e., the best thing available, not more than just that.

Another point to keep in mind is that it is easier to explain growth once it is happening and to explain wealth once it has been achieved then to actually forecast or trigger growth. Nevertheless, in particular the more recent growth stories of the "Asian tigers" do seem to give clear hints how growth can be "created", including through active government interference. Lessons can be learned from these stories, but each country and each situation has it specificities. The economic discipline is not a "hard" science and economic growth cannot be produced in the way a building is constructed or a bridge. To conclude it may be useful to add that the meaning and the measurement of practically any social data, GDP to begin with, let alone "the rule of law", always contain a degree of uncertainty and inaccuracy, which further complicate the exercise. However, we do have hints, indicators, hypotheses and pointers.

Chapter II

The West Competing
with Low-Wage China

II.1. China's Bilateral Trade Surplus with the EU and the US: One Big Difference

For the economist bilateral trade deficits or surpluses do not matter. With certain countries we run surpluses, with others, deficits. That is the whole idea of the international division of labour and international trade. In the same vein, I have a "deficit" with my supermarket and my bookstore, but a "surplus" with my employer. What counts is the overall trade balance, or more correctly the current account balance of a country (or other type of economic area, the Euro-zone, for instance). In the long run (large) deficits are unsustainable unless they are compensated by net capital imports — someone has to pay the bill. Without such compensation, in the long term deficits have to be remedied by a depreciation of the currency of an economy to restore what we call "competitiveness" (example: the US today; depreciation = a country lowers its prices). Also huge surpluses are unsustainable in the long run unless they are compensated by net capital exports. If they are not a country should appreciate its currency (= raise its prices). If trade surpluses are not mitigated by net capital exports or a currency appreciation the economy runs the risk of overheating (excessive demand, inflation etc.; example: China today).

A particular aspect comes into play in the case of the growing bilateral trade deficit the EU has with China. Whereas China's exports to and trade surplus with the EU have been rising, the exports of China, Japan, Korea, Taiwan, and ASEAN *combined* have remained a steady 32 percent of the EU's total imports in the last decade. This is not a pure statistical coincidence, but the reflection of the fact that Asian companies outside China use China as the last part of the assembly line for a host of sophisticated products. The share of Chinese value added in these "Chinese" exports is often low, not more than 25 percent (the latter figure also demonstrates the relative value of a gross export figure, because it represents total *gross value* whereas GDP figures represent *value added*).

What is then the problem the US and the EU have with their, true, high and rising bilateral trade deficits with China? The EU trade deficit with China was: 50 billion euro in 2005 and 100 euro and 180 billion euro in 2006 and 2007. Chinese officials like to mention and hail the "ever rising amount of our bilateral trade". "Yes, but you have a much better part of the deal" is the sour answer from their European and American counterparts and who can blame the latter for that answer? Both the US and the EU accuse China of unfair trade practices, such as discriminating against foreign companies when it comes to access for to the Chinese markets (both for EU and US exporters and investors), theft of intellectual property, subsidizing Chinese state-owned companies and not least (more in particular the US, but more recently the EU too) of "manipulating" its currency.

The EU and the US are on many accounts right. The issue is about trade policy and a lack of openness of the Chinese market for products and investment from the EU and the US. The international trade game has rules with the World Trade Organization as the arbiter. The US has, so far, more often than the EU submitted cases against China to the WTO. Such a submission leads to a long bureaucratic process, however. The EU has been more active in trying to find solutions through bilateral talks with China. The most publicised bilateral deal concluded with China was the Memorandum of Understanding on China's textiles exports, of September 2005. It was the armistice so to say of what media dubbed as the "bra war".

Does China manipulate its currency? It has pegged, since 2005 "loosely" pegged, its currency to the USD and received praise for this until 2003. I say loosely pegged, because in spite of the official announcement, in June 2005, that the link with the USD would be abandoned, the Chinese currency seems to have continued to follow the USD fairly closely, in particular, in the first six months after the announcement. However, by the middle of 2008, i.e., two-and-a-half years after the Chinese announced their "de-pegging" the value of the Chinese renminbi had increased by 21 percent against the USD. But for the time being this is the reflection of dollar weakness, not renminbi strength. In June 2008, the Chinese renminbi had fallen by 10 percent since June 2005 against the rising euro. This latter fact is often overlooked by the US oriented financial analysts and media.

"Pegging" is "regulating", which in a more pejorative sense can be called "manipulating". The International Monetary Fund (IMF) and other research suggests, and a number of other analysts agree, that the Chinese currency may still be undervalued by something between 30 percent and 40 percent (February 2008). But there is also fairly conclusive research that even if such an increase of the renminbi exchange rate were to happen this fact by itself might do little to stop a further increase of the surpluses China has in its trade with the EU and the US. So far Chinese exports have indeed remained strong in spite of wage and price rises in China (which imply a real appreciation of the renminbi through higher renminbi prices) and the strengthening of the Chinese currency against the US dollar.

On the currency issue the EU's message to China in the last few years has been: "It would be *in your own interest* if you allowed greater flexibility in your exchange rate market." In particular in early 2008, with rising inflation and wages in China and an ever increasing trade surplus, leading existing global imbalances to continue and even widen, the most obvious textbook solution to re-balancing the situation for Chinese policy makers would indeed be to let the exchange rate go up. Finally, in 2008 Chinese monetary decision makers seemed to be prepared to go ahead into this direction with greater determination.

The EU believes — and stresses this more than the US does — that apart from the exchange rate, re-balancing should also be achieved by *further structural change* in China. China has a savings rate which is higher than ever seen in Asia's other fast growing countries — which were already high by international standards. Reform, for instance, of China's health care system could lead to a better balanced situation. After the collapse of the state health care system, health care costs are high for individual Chinese citizens and, consequently, drive up saving by households who seek to cover the risk they run.[29] The same can be said for China's social security system. A "consumption boom" by China's growing middle class could ease the problem as it should lead to higher Chinese imports. Such a boom has been predicted for a number of years now and, once again, in 2008, but it hasn't come as yet.

There is one important difference between the bilateral trade deficit of the US with China and the EU one. The US has a big *overall* trade deficit, whereas the EU has not. In the first months of 2008, the EU continued to have an insignificant current account deficit, for the Euro-zone it was zero. In spite of concerns about the US economy and the possibility of a spill-over to the rest of the world, unemployment in the Euro-zone was at a 25-year low in early 2008 (admittedly, confidence indicators were falling though). Could it be that cheap Chinese inputs have helped European producers to stay competitive in spite of the ever rising euro? Could it be that Chinese inputs have helped the European economy tick? Moreover, in the EU both monetary and fiscal policymakers have sailed a more cautious course than their American counterparts in the last years. The policy of the European Central Bank (ECB) has sometimes been criticised as too conservative, but for the time being it seems to work. And after years of struggling with government debt EU Member States now try to outdo each other by presenting balanced government budgets. A budget deficit of more than 3 percent of GDP is considered "excessive" and puts the EU Member State concerned under scrutiny by the European Commission.[30]

---

[29] With every single household having to set aside money for possible future risks much bigger amounts are involved than with the "spread" properly run health care systems provide for.

[30] The official ("headline") US budget deficit figure for 2007 is 2.4 percent of GDP. But the website of the US Treasury shows debt of USD 9.2 trillion on 31 December 2007 and 8.6 trillion on 31/12/2006, an increase of 0.6 trillion, 4.5 percent of US GDP.

The US, on the other hand, has a large *overall* current account *deficit* — of 5 percent of US GDP in 2007, which was not decreasing in early 2008. Much more than the EU the US needs a "culprit" and who can be more easily pointed at than China? China seems, however, the *consequence* of the US's problem rather than the cause. Underlying America's trade deficit is its extremely low savings rate with the trade deficit as its mirror image. America's loose, if not reckless monetary policy (and to a certain extent perhaps its loose fiscal policy too) by Federal Reserve Chairman Greenspan — policies which were subsequently backed up by his successor Bernanke when the US economy had, once again, to be steered away from slowdown — have led to this situation to continue.[31] The US trade deficit has to a large extent been *made in USA*, and should probably also be repaired there.

"Come back in a year from now" the sceptical observer may say. The economic profession remains a tricky business. But at the time of writing, the first half of 2008, it is difficult to see how the US dollar could go up and quite easy how it may go further down.[32] The most logical course of events would seem a higher yuan and a lower dollar. At the same time, short-term recession worries aside, *long-term* prospects for the EU economy are better than they have been for many years. For 15 years the EU has been urging the former planned economies that finally joined the EU in 2004 and 2007 to reform and they did, thoroughly. At the same time it took Germany some 25 years of political debate to extend the opening hours of shops on Saturday afternoons. But today there seems to be a real readiness for reform to be emerging, also in "old" Europe. Moreover, many of the Member States that joined since 2004, although poorer than the 15 "old ones", seem to have increased the dynamism of the EU economy as a whole.

---

[31] In his "*The Age of Turbulence*", 2007, Mr. Greenspan criticizes Mr. Bush's fiscal policy. But when he was in function — when it might still have mattered — he ducked questions on the subject during his hearings with Congress. By doing so he *de facto* gave Bush's fiscal policy his blessing.

[32] In 2002 the USD stood at 1.12 against the euro; in September 2007 at USD 1.41 against the euro; it *might* go down further to 2.00 against the euro; it may seem unlikely, but nobody knows.

Perspective: The economies of the EU and the US are roughly of the same size, the EU economy is slightly larger. Population sizes are 300 million and 500 million respectively, GDP per head at PPP is 33,000 USD in the EU and 46,000 in the US (40 percent higher). Part of the explanation for this gap is that the EU recently took 12 new countries on board most of them much poorer than the 15 "old" ones. Another part is that the proportion of Americans who work is higher than of Europeans who work. In addition, working Americans work many more hours per year than their European counterparts. Output per person per hour in the "old" EU (of 15 Member States, before 2004) is more or less similar to that in the US. In the US income inequalities are much larger than in the EU (Gini coefficients are 45 and 31 respectively[33]). The EU and the US have both considerable trade deficits with China, in 2007 these deficits were 180 billion euro and 250 billion USD respectively and they are increasingly becoming a political problem. The signs are, however, that these deficits peaked already and that they may ease in the medium term.

II.2. Are Jobs and Wages in the West at Risk?

In the previous sub-chapter (II.1) I have argued that bilateral trade or current account deficits are of limited economic relevance, although they may lead to political concern. But what is the impact of the rise of China (and India and Asia in general) on what matters most: jobs and wages, both in the West and in these emerging economies? Until some twenty years ago, workers from rich countries used to have monopoly access to Western capital. However, with capital and knowledge and technology now easily travelling, China's (and India's or Asia's) "reserve army of labour" is able to compete with Western labour — in a way which has somewhat "the same effect as mass

---

[33] To give an idea: Coefficients for Brazil, China, India and Sweden are 57, 47, 37 and 23 respectively.

migration of this reserve army to the rich countries would have" (as economist Paul Samuelson puts it).

The Dutch government office for economic analysis (CPB) has tried to quantify the precise "China effect" for the Dutch economy. The CPB analysis gives a rosy picture of 35,000 jobs created in the Netherlands due to the China factor ("thank you, China" were media reactions based on CPB's upbeat press release when the study was issued).[34] However, a closer look shows that the CPB, which is well-known for its sophisticated economic model analysis of the Dutch economy, has not done its analysis of the China factor in an equally sophisticated way. What has been calculated, concerns jobs created in the "China shop" of the Dutch economy, i.e., jobs in harbours, sales, repackaging and other activities directly related to Chinese imports into the Netherlands (a substantial part of these imports is further transferred to other countries).

Another factor, somewhat superficially estimated is the des-inflationary effect cheap Chinese imports have had on prices, leading to higher real incomes and lower interest rates. Not accounted for in the CPB analysis are jobs that may have disappeared due to competition from China and therefore the *net* effect on jobs or the impact on wages. When I asked, the authors of the study about this omission they replied that the first question (jobs) was too complicated. The answer to the second question (incomes) was that the income distribution in the Netherlands had remained unchanged in the last five years. That may be true, but without wage competition from China, the income distribution might have become more equal in these last five years.

In a chapter of "Dancing with Giants" the authors estimate the longer term effect of the rise of China and India on the world economy as a whole within the framework of the Global Trade Analysis Project (GTAP), a general equilibrium model. It is a more ambitious and more insightful approach than the CPB exercise, but also a more theoretical one (less based on empirical data). The resulting figures, interesting as they may be, are entirely the result of the

---

[34] CPB, China and the Dutch economy, 2006.

underlying assumptions and hence should be seen as no more than a *possible scenario*. The approach taken, has, however, the advantage of including all elements of the equation and ensuring coherence and consistency between the various outcomes: "increased exports from one country must be accommodated by increased imports by other countries and broad-based increases in productivity that raise competitiveness also raise factor prices and help offset the original increase in competitiveness".[35]

It is calculated that by 2020 the *overall* effect of China's and India's rise on the economies of the EU and the US is *practically nil*. In certain sectors the effect may be considerable, though. The largest individual sector effects in both the EU and the US are in apparel, where a 10 percent decline is expected. The single largest sector losses world-wide are seen in Africa (25 percent loss in the electronics sector) and Philippines (25 percent in apparel). The reader should note that these figures are not about actual decline, but "less than baseline", i.e., how much lower than it would have been otherwise — without the China and India effect.

These model calculations demonstrate that we can see what is increasing or gone or going in sectors *known today*, but also, that we can't see what is around the corner. Reductions in existing sectors are specified to one decimal point, but *new* sectors where new employment should be emerging are not, in fact cannot, be identified by the model. Because it is assumed that Western economies will continue growing and other economies too by the way, by implication employment will (have to) be created somewhere. So far, that has been what is happening since the beginning of the industrial revolution.

Employment in the West (the rich countries) is disappearing in a number of sectors, notably manufacturing, but also certain service sectors (blacksmiths, for instance) — a fact which is widely publicised on each occasion that a factory closes — but in the first quarter of 2008, in spite of recession noises in the US, unemployment in the Euro-zone was at a 25-year low and employment has been increasing

---

[35] B. Dimaranan, E. Ianchovichina, W. Martin: "Competing with Giants: who wins, who loses?" in "*Dancing with Giants*".

as new companies and sectors emerge. The virtues and values of SMEs (Small and Medium sized Enterprises) are often sung. No doubt SMEs are an important part of the cardio-vascular system that keeps the bloodstream of the business sector going. One point rarely mentioned with regard to SMEs is the simple and obvious, if not banal, fact that all private companies that are large today, from General Electric to Google and from Unilever to Lenovo, once were small or medium sized. For having companies, any company, to grow into large companies one day the inflow of small companies has to continue.

It has to be borne in mind that the model calculations referred to above concern only the *trade* effect of China and India. This trade effect aside, the fear is often expressed that capital will be drawn to low-wage countries jobs will be moved abroad and rich economies will be "hollowed out". There are, however, limits to how far this process can go on. A basic identity of economics states:

$$\text{Savings–Investment} = \text{Exports–Imports}^{36}$$

For instance, China's huge trade surplus (Exports–Imports) — in 2007 at 10 percent of its GDP — is the reflection of the Chinese tendency to save a lot, in fact an unprecedented proportion of 50 percent of GDP is saved, more than the already very high investment ratio of 40 percent of GDP. At the same time the US's trade deficit, of 5 percent of its GDP, is the result of a very low savings rate and a modest investment ratio. China's high trade surplus along with high investment is causing pressure on China's economic capacity. It is expected that China's high trade surpluses will disappear, or fall at least, once China's growing middle class starts consuming and, consequently, the saving rate will come down.

If investment from rich countries is pouring in unlimited and provided that savings come down at a given moment the left hand of the

---

[36] National income Y can be defined either as $Y = C + I + X - M$ (income equals what is received from Consumption, Investment and eXports after deduction of money spent on iMports); or as $Y = C + S$ (income is either Saved or Consumed); combining these two equations gives $S = I + X - M$ or $S - I = X - M$.

equation (Saving–Investment) has to become negative. But then, by definition the right hand should become negative too (as said, the equation states an identity), i.e., imports should exceed exports (because consumers in the low-wage country have increased consumption). So the conclusion has to be that the dislocation of production capacity from rich countries to low-wage countries cannot co-exist with continuous trade deficits in rich countries.

The experience of the 1930's when countries increased import barriers after initially a period of globalisation followed by the depression that set in 1929 seems to tell us that in spite of the pain competition may cause, the introduction of protective measures is not the way out. Nevertheless, when capital is free to go where it wants to, as it is today (much more so than several decades ago), labour in both Europe and the US is indeed in competition with the "reserve army of labour" in China and other Asian and non-Asian low-wage countries in its quest for capital. So the conclusion can only be that, yes, the "China factor" and globalisation will affect jobs and wages, i.e., (part of) jobs will move abroad and jobs that stay in the EU and the US may be less well paid. Even staunch pro-globalisation author Martin Wolf admits that this can be the case.[37] However, he says, capital continues to go predominantly to richer nations, conclusion: this competition is not that much of a problem. Fine, not today, one may react, but what will be the situation in 10 or 20 years from now?

The most obvious answer is that the examples of Japan, Korea and Taiwan have shown, as other economies before them,[38] that as economies emerge, productivity and wages rise — like productivity and wages are rising in China today. Annual wage rises in China have been of the order of 14 percent in the last few years, much higher than the increase of productivity, which means that unit labour costs in China are rising. We saw already that China's currency has been rising in the last few years, albeit mostly against the sinking US dollar and not (yet?) for instance against the strongly rising euro.

---

[37] M. Wolf, *Why Globalization Works*, 2004.
[38] Including Germany for instance at a much earlier stage.

The pressure to improve productivity increases as labour shortages are reported in management and other professional functions.
The "reserve army" of young, flexible and easy-to-move workers
from China's rural areas is drying up, which is one of the reasons
that certain companies move from China's coastal areas to the
Western part of the country — which raises transport costs, however — or to India, Indonesia or Vietnam. That China's prices are
gradually rising is, for instance, also admitted by Alexandra Harney
after some two hundred pages of "China Price" drumbeat. The
"China price" story, popular in the US, can be summarised as: low
labour standards, lack of workers' rights and competition for jobs
drive labour costs down, is this fair? Perhaps not, but when productivity rises and the pool of labour dries up, wages and related
labour costs will eventually go up — as they have always done,
everywhere. Also Harney admits: "Ultimately, however, this kind
of individual rights awareness has an effect that is at once prosaic
and momentous: *It makes China more like other countries* (emphasis
mine)".[39] And that is exactly the point. Today it is China, yesterday
it was Japan. This conclusion does not come as a surprise when one
considers the "China Price" in the wider context of world-wide
economic development and emerging economies in the last few
centuries. The pattern is repeated over and over again or as Paul
Krugman puts it:

> Economic history offers no example of a country that experience
> long-term productivity growth without a roughly equal rise in real
> wages. In the 1950s, when European productivity was typically less
> than half of US productivity, so were European wages; today aver-
> age compensation measured in dollars is about the same. As Japan
> climbed the productivity ladder over the past 30 years, its wages also
> rose, from 10 percent to 110 percent of the US level. South Korea's
> wages have also risen dramatically over time.[40]

---

[39] A. Harvey, *The China Price*, 2008.
[40] P. Krugman, *Pop Internationalism*, 1996.

The most likely scenario is that in 10, 20 or 30 years from now China and India and other nations which are about to join the ranks of Middle Lower Income countries will have lost their special position in the same manner as Japan has. Barring major disruptions to the global economic system these economies will be fully incorporated in the global market system by then. Wage levels in these economies will have gone up, together with increased productivity, and be comparable with wage and productivity levels in the economies that are rich today or they will be approaching these levels. Investment flows will go both ways,[41] China is already turning into an exporter of capital (not net though). Moreover, to qualify the "hollowing out" thesis further, with more than 70 percent of jobs in the rich economies in the services sector, not all jobs can be moved abroad.

How about wages and incomes in the West? Thorough analysis of developments in *the distribution of incomes* is reported about in the World Bank's World Economic Outlook,[42] based on a comparison of a variety of research sources. While stressing the many caveats, because of uncertainty surrounding data and the precise causes and effects with so many things happening at the same time, the conclusion is that in the last two decades the following developments can be seen:

- First, income differences *between* countries would have *decreased* — as poorer countries catch up (not least China and India)
- Second, inequality *within* countries would have *increased*. However, *technology* would be a more important factor at work here than globalisation (this is an important finding as it would suggest that something can be done by upgrading the workforce and improving labour's versatility)
- Third, insofar as globalisation is the cause of greater inequality, the international investment factor ("they steal our jobs") would

---

[41] This is assuming that investment from emerging countries can go where it wants and is not discriminated against (an assumption that can not be taken for granted given the discrimination even *within* the EU, with Italy and France as the most protectionist and more in general against "non-white" capital in the West).

[42] World Development Report 2007, "*Globalization and Inequality*".

have a stronger effect than trade ("we have to go out of business, because they over flood our market")

The technology factor indicates, once again, that training and re-training of the labour force are important, more important than pro-tective measures. Exact analysis and assessment of the various factors at work is complicated, but two more aspects should be mentioned. First, a job may be moved abroad together with new technology, i.e., the factory put up in say China may be more modern than the old one closed in Europe or the US. Second, "moved abroad" relates to invest-ment by Western capital (or capital from rich Asian economies, with Japan, Taiwan and Korea most prominent among them[43]) in low-wage countries leading to the loss of specific jobs in richer economies.

There are estimates that more than 50 percent of China's exports are the result of foreign investment in China. The fact is sometimes stressed by the Chinese side when China is accused of unfair trade prac-tices: "these are your own companies". This is the notion that we are "competing with ourselves" and that, therefore, there is nothing to worry about. Among those who want us to see it this way I take G.J. Gilboy as an example. In an article in "Foreign Affairs" — which he wrote when he was a "senior manager at a major multinational firm in Beijing" according to a footnote to the article — he paints a cheerful picture of the wonderful investment opportunities China offers to American investors[44] and how well US and American interests interact (the EU and Japan are mentioned once in his article and in passing only). Gilboy leaves the reader with one big unanswered question, how-ever: what is in it for workers, other than buying the cheaper products?

Let me reiterate that in all, in spite of (or thanks to?) the China fac-tor and in spite of a record high euro, unemployment in the EU was at a 25 year low until May 2008, when signs of an economic slowdown in the EU following the slowing of the US economy, became ever more apparent and unemployment edged up. At the end

---

[43] Estimates of Taiwanese investment in mainland China vary from 60 billion to 150 billion USD.

[44] George J. Gilboy, "The myth behind China's miracle", in *Foreign Affairs*, July/August 2004.

of April 2008, in spite of gloomy, not-so-rosy outlook for the German economy as a whole, German market research institute GFK reported that German consumer confidence was *up*.[45] In the same vein, until recession noises began to emerge in the US, at the end of 2007, also US unemployment was low. In the 1990's the US Federal Reserve Board adhered to a new productivity paradigm, resulting from assumptions about technological progress and the theory was that unemployment could be lower than before without leading to higher inflation. The possibility that imports from low-wage countries might have led to this novel situation was not mentioned. The, admittedly tentative, conclusions that can be drawn are that globalisation, the China factor and open borders have for a long time led to the following:

- The availability of relatively cheap industrial products, cheaper than they would have been otherwise, for Western consumers and, consequently, an overall effect of reducing inflation (the cost of living);
- Greater investment possibilities for Western capital and, consequently, higher profits;
- Greater pressure on wages/incomes in the West, in particular for unskilled or less skilled labour and, consequently, lower wages (or wage increases which are lower than they would have been otherwise); but economic analysis is unable to fully distinguish between technology and the effect of competition from low-wage countries (whether through trade or investment);
- Higher prices for resources, from oil and other raw materials to food; this latter trend, not generally predicted, has become particularly visible in the course of 2007.

II.3. What Is It: Low-Wage Countries or Technology; or Both?

In particular American authors and politicians have produced an impressive flood of print on the "they steal our jobs" theme. Let me

---

[45] www.gfk.com/group.

take as an example "Myths of Free Trade" by American Congressman Sherrod Brown who puts the blame of government's failure to stop cheap imports on "corporate lobbies". Brown introduces laid-off steelworker Rich Littleton who laments "I'm 38 years old. How marketable am I? (...) I always wanted to do the same thing my father did." Littleton furthermore laments that not only his father, but also both his grandfathers had worked in the steel mill concerned in Ohio Valley, which had laid off almost a quarter of its 4,000 employees. Whether these jobs were made redundant by new technology or steel imports from low-wage countries or for other reasons, is not explained. Apparently, globalisation is automatically assumed guilty.

Another thing strikes as odd in this description although I don't think it was Brown's intention. It is the unspoken acceptance of the fact that it is entirely normal for a supposedly mentally and physically healthy person living in 1998 at the age of 38 to hope, even expect to do "the same thing" his father and two grandfathers did. Should we understand that notions like 'technological change" and "economic progress" are unknown to Mr. Littleton and Mr. Brown? Would Mr. Littleton also have accepted the living conditions of his ancestors? What to think of a 38-year-old who complains about his marketability in what is, we are told, the most flexible economy of the world and the most mobile labour force on earth?

I cannot resist to point at an inconsistency in Brown's logic when he turns from steel to pharmaceuticals, because it so marvellously reveals the flaw in the protectionist argument. That flaw is that protectionism may protect a steel employer or steelworker here or there, but in the end it always means a burden, a tax, on citizens who have demonstrated a preference to buy "next door". After first siding with his laid off steelworker Brown scolds corporate lobbyists and Washington politicians for *not* allowing cheap pharmaceutical imports into America. Brown laments that this fact to *higher prices* for medicines in the US (what else could we expect?): "Never passing up a chance to assist the nation's drug companies, the Bush administration used the 2003 Medicare legislation to discourage less expensive mail or order drugs and senior citizen bus trips to Canada (*which I arranged in my district* — emphasis mine) to buy prescription drugs."

Apparently Brown is not against all cheap imports. Cheap medicines are right, cheap steel is wrong. I can only conclude that there are steelworkers, but no pharmaceutical firms or pharmaceutical workers in Congressman Brown's constituency, but *users* of medicines there are without doubt. And apparently the voice of steel consumers, who one can expect to be there too, is less well heard than the voice of steel workers and the voice of pharmaceuticals consumers.

The dilemma so beautifully expressed here by the author, in his innocence, is, as I pointed out before, that globalisation is (in principle and others things equal) "good" for consumers (greater choice, cheaper products), "good" for the owners of mobile capital (greater choice, higher profits), and can be "bad" for labour if it is immobile and inflexible and cannot adjust. A dilemma indeed, because it is not only about competition between classes of people, but also because most of us are, in varying degrees and often at the same time consumers, workers — one more versatile and less affected by competition from technology or far away countries than the other — and investors too (everybody who participates in a funded pension scheme is knowingly or not an investor and benefits from higher returns on capital).

In addition to the *dilemma* we may often be faced with, there is an information and perception problem, which tends to overstate the "competitive threat" side of the equation. Media report about factories that are closed and sudden lay-offs of a certain importance. But news about jobs that are created goes by unnoticed. "General Electric cuts 10,000 jobs" or "Nokia moves 3,000 jobs from Germany to Romania" makes headlines. But the fact, for instance, that in the period 2004 to 2007 IBM created 90,000 jobs worldwide has gone by practically unnoticed by media. And so does the on-going hiring of staff by small and medium sized companies A, B to Z, all taken together adding up to thousands of jobs. On 23 April 2008, financial headlines flashed another "all-time low" of the US dollar against the euro (1.60 USD for 1 euro this time) and the risk this implies for EU competitiveness. Another hot news item that day was about, once again, new write-offs by banks because of the US made subprime crisis.

On the same day, a short article on page 4 of the Financial Times reported about the German Engineering Association whose members, in particular SME companies, saw their *biggest boom in 40 years.*[46] The Association — indeed, not one particular company — just had lifted its forecast for the number of jobs to be created this year in the sector, indeed not all in one go, from 10,000 to 30,000. The dollar/euro exchange rate would soon be back in the news and so would new details about the subprime crisis, the forecast of the German Engineering Association would not.

The reason for this bias is that "news" usually is bad news. News is by definition about traffic accidents, fires and bad weather, not about travellers who have arrived safely, buildings that did not go up in flames and beautiful weather. A second reason is that unions from the logic of the role they have to play tend to issue statements or take action when factories are closed and jobs are cut, not when factories are opened and new people hired. Today it may be authoritarian regimes or local authorities rather who still make a big issue of festive plant openings, but the practice seems to be getting more and more out of fashion.

An even more important factor complicating the picture is technological progress. This aspect is well covered in the economic literature, but less so in the media, probably in part because the precise effect of technology can prove very difficult to measure. Continuous technological progress leads to higher productivity and, consequently, higher wages and incomes, but also, inevitably, to certain *specific* jobs disappearing (and, on the other hand, new ones emerging). Manufacturing output in the US and Germany has been rising steadily, for decades on, but at the same time jobs in manufacturing have been on a steady, also decade-long decline in both countries.

The more productivity increases the fewer workers will be needed to produce the same amount of output and with productivity growing further fewer will be needed, even to produce more output. This has nothing to do with China, India or other low-wage countries. Moreover,

---

[46] Financial Times, 23/04/08:"The subprime crisis is not noticeable to us at all. We are in the biggest boom since the end of the 1960s".

in spite of all the lamenting and alarmist stories the US's share in world manufacturing output has remained unchanged for more than a decade. According to the US Cato Institute, citing the United Nations Industrial Development Organization, the US share of world manufacturing, in terms of value-added, was 21.1 percent in 2005 against 21.4 percent in 1993. Over the same period the EU saw its share declining from 29.3 percent to 26.5 percent, Japan's share would have gone down from 22.4 percent to 19 percent and China's up from 3.5 percent in 1993 to 8 percent in 2005.[47] As the Cato Institute put it in another study[48]:

> "But declining employment in a sector that is producing record output is hardly credible evidence of doom. In fact, the two indicators taken together are evidence of soaring labor productivity, which is the source of long-term increases in living standards. With the national unemployment rate at 4.5 percent, 1.8 million net new jobs created on average every year since 1980, U.S. plants producing record output, and manufacturing companies earning record profits, what is so troubling about the loss of manufacturing jobs?"

The crucial thing is that technological progress requires labour to adapt, learn new skills and take on jobs that may not have existed before, sometimes in the same sector of activity or related sectors, sometimes in other sectors. *I don't exclude and in fact my hypothesis is that in the EU labour's capacity to adapt is greater than in the US and that this is more in particular the case for low skilled labour.* The reason is, I think and I will elaborate on this point later, that whereas top quality education in the US is probably still the best available (and at least among the best available) in the world, in the EU access to decent levels of education, both professional and general, below that absolute top is greater than in the US. More modest (lower quality) skills and knowledge are wider spread among the population as a

---

[47] Bhagyashree Garekar, US manfacturers "don't need protection", *Straits Times*, 30 May, 2008.
[48] Daniel Ikenson, *Talk About Industry's Demise Just a Manufactured Myth*, Cato Institute, November, 2007.

whole in the EU than in the US and, consequently, adaptability at the lower end of the skills scale is in the EU greater than in the US.

In the case of the Mr. Middleton, whom we met above, as in the case of so many insufficiently skilled workers, it is practically impossible to identify exactly whether their jobs have become redundant because of technology or competition from low-wage countries, both factors combined or other factors in addition. Italy is an example of a EU Member State which, in spite of examples of impressive technological and commercial achievements, struggles with a vast army of graduates in philosophy, the arts and other related subjects who, by lack of adaptability, are unable to fit jobs that are available and therefore are only able to find low-paid jobs with requirements below their capacities.

Suppose that it would be possible to distinguish between and separate the effects of technology and low-wage countries respectively, would it make much difference either for those concerned or for policy makers? Does it matter from a policy point of view? In a sense it is as counterproductive — and in the long-term as much to the detriment of further growth of productivity and living standards — to limit imports from China and other low-wage countries as it would be counterproductive and detrimental to tax or otherwise hinder technological development. Taxing or otherwise hindering technological progress, a policy once supported in Marxist circles, is no longer an option that is given serious consideration in countries with serious policies to foster economic growth.[49] But until today taxing or otherwise hindering imports from low-wage countries has many supporters, is applied and extending its reach and is still receiving serious consideration as a policy option. In fact, we have not that much to conclude thus far. The few points we have gathered are:

- Bilateral trade deficits have limited economic meaning, if any;
- It is difficult, if not impossible, to quantify accurately the effect of low-wage countries (China, India, Asia) on jobs and wages in rich

---

[49] This policy was applied by many developing countries (including China and India), which after colonialism adhered to "self-subsistence" ("sorry, no trade please"), which in the end appeared to serve them badly.

countries; both international competition *and* technological progress create a dynamic ever-changing environment in which it is hard to distinguish the precise effect of each factor;

- Training and re-training of the labour force is crucial;
- Our perception is blurred by what we see and what we don't see: jobs that disappear are better seen than newly created jobs.

II.4. Globalisation: South/North Divide in the EU, Left/Right in the US

When we compare the attitude towards low-wage countries and possible protectionist measures in the EU and the US there is a noticeable difference. In the US concerns about the "China threat" or free trade usually come from politicians of the Democratic Party and union leaders. To put it simply, in the US protectionism versus free trade, including the "China threat" is a "left/right" issue. Free trade, including China, is first and foremost seen as a threat to jobs and when jobs are in danger the Democrats and the unions come to the rescue (or say they will). Whatever arguments about the role of technology are brought to the table, first and foremost free trade and China are seen as labour's enemy. In the EU, on the other hand, it is much more a North versus South issue. Let me clarify.

In March and April 2008, the two democratic candidates for the race for the US White House, Clinton and Obama, both found it necessary to expose their protectionist credentials by promising a review of the North American Free Trade Agreement (NAFTA), America's free trade agreement with Canada and Mexico this time, but China fits in the same "threat" category. This NAFTA review promise by both candidates seemed unrealistic and hardly credible, but both candidates apparently felt that they needed this argument to improve their chances among voters in the Democratic Primaries. This so in spite of the fact that what they felt urged to promise was unlikely ever to be seriously considered were either of them to be elected president. From a global or globaliser's point of view there were more depressing messages from the US campaign trail. On 1 May, Singapore's Straits Times reported that Democratic candidate Hillary Clinton was slowly but steadily crawling back and gaining votes in the Democratic primaries, not only on the race issue (as against her Democratic candidate Barack Obama, a man of colour), but also by playing on "voter fears about globalisation and job losses in troubled industries".[50]

In the EU no mainstream politician, either left or right from the centre, would during an election campaign suggest that *trade* provisions existing *within* the EU (I stress this "within" point because of the NAFTA issue in the US context) should be revised and tariffs or other barriers be re-established. But more significant is that for mainstream parties China or free trade is not a general campaign issue — that is: until now, who knows what next year will bring? Protectionist eruptions occur, but when they do every now and these relate to the free circulation of labour and capital rather, both within and from outside the EU, and are as often (if not more often) expressed by those on the right side of the political spectre as on the left side. In certain quarters of the EU there are of course forceful voices against globalisation and economic integration in all its forms, including integration within Europe.[51] These voices are, however, from groups of limited size at both the utter left or utter right side of the political spectrum where ultra-left or communism and the anti-capitalist ultra-right meet, not mainstream parties or major unions.

In March 2008, at a summit meeting of EU political leaders the question of globalisation, jobs and employment in the EU took centre stage and options were discussed of which attitude to take and which policies to follow. Two documents prepared for that summit broadly reflect my point. These documents express by implication the positions in mainstream Europe on the question of globalisation, low-wage countries (China) and technological progress. One of the documents was issued by the European Trade Union Confederation (ETUC)[52] under the title "Quality of Jobs at Risk!" The other document, more business oriented or "business leaning", was "The European

---

[50] Derwin Pereira, (Singapore's) Straits Times, 1 May, 2008.

[51] These may include calls for closing the French border for Spanish "imports", as if California were to close its borders for "imports" from other parts of the US.

[52] ETUC, Quality of Jobs at Risk; ETUC is also known under its name in French, which is Confédération européenne des syndicates (CES).

Growth and Jobs Monitor, 2008", issued by "the Lisbon Council", a think–tank that seeks to provide follow–up to the commitment made by EU political leaders at their Summit in Lisbon in March 2000, which led to the "Lisbon Agenda".

In the TUC (trade unions) document there is no word on China or low-wage countries, let alone EU integration. The document contains one reference to "a globalising world". The main concerns expressed by the Union of EU trade unions relate to the quality of jobs and job security. True, employers are called upon to improve job quality and job security. To put it very simply: in the US China and low-wage countries more in general are labour's adversary, in the EU employers or capital is. In the second document, as in the former, globalisation is mentioned, albeit it almost in passing, but China and India or other specific low-wage countries are not. The issues dealt with in The European Growth and Jobs Monitor are just that, growth and jobs, and how to get more of both of them, through the improvement of productivity, human capital, investment, sustainable public finances and energy efficiency. The focus is on what we ourselves should do to do things better and not how should we stop others from doing what they do.

A closer look at differences of opinion on the China (low-wage/globalisation) question as expressed in the EU shows as I mentioned a marked *North/South divide*. Worries about competition from China are expressed not by "the left", but by political leaders and employers in Member States on the Southern edge of the EU. Italy, Greece and Portugal as the clearest examples, are the most persistent and outspoken. Depending on the issues at stake, Spain and France may join this "club of protectionists". On several occasions when the EU was considering and debating the possibility of protectionist measures against products from China — textiles in 2005, shoes in 2006 — the North/South divide has become very visible.

The North/South divide — once again, not concerning China only, but free trade more in general — was also reflected by an action of Sweden's conservative trade minister Bjorling in March 2008. She announced she wanted to rally pro-free trade *countries* in the European Union against what she saw "as a better organised protectionist camp" (of countries) in the EU. "We have seen more and more EU countries getting together among the protectionists. It's scary for us as the watchdogs of free trade." The minister had had talks, she said, with the UK, the Czech Republic, Denmark, Estonia, Latvia and Lithuania. The role of Germany in this possible free-traders camp in the making remained unclear, although Germany usually is among the "free-traders", and somewhat surprisingly in-principle-free-traders the Netherlands and Finland were not included in the minister's list, but this latter fact may have been a simple omission.[53]

For further illustration of the North/South divide in the EU one may look at poll figures about the public perception of China in various EU Member States. In late March/early April, 2008, the answer to the question "do you see China as a threat?" was "yes" for 47 percent of Italians, 36 percent of French, 35 percent of Germans and 27 percent of those polled in the UK. The figures were on average 16 percent lower in June 2007 (26 percent, 22 percent, 18 percent and 16 percent for Italy, France, Germany and the UK respectively). The large increase within one year should probably mostly if not entirely be explained by the fact that the April 2008 poll was taken just after unrest in Tibet began, which received wide media coverage, and during the early stage of the infamous Olympic Torch Relay, which led to the emergence of fierce nationalist sentiment in China.[54] So these percentages, in particular those of the March/April poll, reflect more than just concerns about competition and trade. This also means that the more negative scores may ease again once (if and when) the effect of the political aspects is to subside. Nevertheless, whatever role the human rights aspect may have played, the order from more to less China fear, highest in Italy, lowest in the UK (only a small number of EU Member States were covered by the poll), remained unchanged between June 2007 and early April 2008.

---

[53] "Sources Say", an internal European Commission News Review and other press coverage, 10 March, 2008.

[54] FT-Harris as published on the internet. "China fear" fear figures for Italy were very close for those in the US. "For the first time, Europeans ranked China as the biggest threat to global stability — ahead of the US, North Korea and Iran (Geoffrey Dyer and John Thornhill, Financial Times, 2/5/08).

The North/South divide in the EU notwithstanding, the question "China: threat or opportunity" seems in general to receive a more optimistic reaction in Europe than in the US. My tentative *explanation* for this consists of a number of factors. These same factors should then also explain, at least in part, why countries on Europe's South flank are more concerned and negative about China — *more "US like"* in this particular respect — than those in the EU's North. What can these factors be?

A first factor might be that individual European countries, in particular the smaller ones, have a much longer history than the US of exposure to and dependence on foreign trade. The US has a history of foreign trade not being more than 10 percent of its GDP. Today, US exports are still 10 percent of its GDP, but imports have risen to 15 percent of GDP (resulting in a trade deficit of 5 percent of GDP). In the smaller Member States of the EU exports (and imports) are very often more than 50 percent of GDP, but even in Germany exports or close to 25 percent of GDP. I consider this factor for the moment as a pure conjecture however, because I have no evidence to argue that history and developments as reflected by these statistics would have a significant effect on the attitudes of politicians or the population.

The second point is much easier to make. The EU has greatly improved its macro-economic position and stability over the last ten years, in particular since the introduction of the Euro. In addition, the enlargements of 2004 and 2007 seem to have improved macro-economic *dynamism* in the EU. In the US, on the other hand, a much less cautious macro-economic policy during the period 2001/2008 has seriously deteriorated macro-economic stability. Would a difference in macro-economic stability be able to explain Europe's North/South difference? If it is an explanatory factor there should be a significant difference in macro-economic performance too when "EU North" and "EU South" are compared.

Third, looking for factors at micro-level, it seems plausible that Europe's more inclusive and egalitarian social model may result in a greater feeling of security among European workers than exists among their US counterparts. This more inclusive European "model" not only leads to a more equal distribution of income,[55] but also to greater access to education of a decent quality and therefore a wider, more equal distribution of knowledge through the population as a whole. If these factors, "security and equality", on the one hand, and "education", on the other, are valid and have an effect they may, first, put EU labour in a more comfortable (more secure) position than US labour and, second, provide EU labour with greater flexibility/adaptability to face competition from China (and globalisation in general). To further the argument OECD research seems to confirm that education systems in EU North give on average better results than in EU South (and the US). If this is indeed the case and, again: there is evidence suggesting this, this difference in quality could help explain the more "US like", more anti-free-trade attitude in EU South.

Fourth, I will compare how individual EU Members and the US respectively score on the report card of the World Bank "good governance" indicators which were discussed before. For support of the hypothesis that the North/South divide in the EU might in part be explained by "governance factors",[56] first, scores for EU Member States should be higher than those for the US and, second, in the EU scores in Northern Member States should be higher than in Southern ones. In the next two sections I will elaborate on these issues.

II.5. Could It Be? The EU Better Placed to Face the Challenge?

II.5.1. *The EU–Lisbon Agenda and Macro-Economic Stability*

It may be useful to remind the reader of the EU Lisbon Agenda of March 2000. This Agenda meant, as it was stated at the time, to improve EU competitiveness by structural reform and the move to a

---

[55] Income inequality as expressed by the Gini coefficient (0 = no inequality at all, 1 = 100 percent inequality: one has all income, the others have nothing) is 0.31 in the EU and 0.46 in the US.
[56] I do not seek to prove the North/South divide in the EU here, which I consider as a political fact. My attempt is a tentative search for underlying economic and social factors, other than trade patterns, explaining this fact.

knowledge–based economy and society; modernise the European social model by investing in people and combating social exclusion together with sound macro-economic policy. In a sense the Lisbon agenda was, if I may put it this way, a commitment by government leaders to "improve public sector performance and stimulate market functioning". In the first five years after 2000 the results of this ambitious agenda were not very impressive and implementation seemed to be lagging. One of the difficulties with the Lisbon Agenda appeared to be that whereas the general commitments had been made at central EU level and were seen by outsiders as EU commitments, policy implementation depended very much on individual Member States. The great plus of the explicit announcement of the Lisbon objectives with considerable fanfare in 2000, was that this made it difficult to forget them. Time and again political leaders in Europe were reminded of the ambitious goals set in 2000, either by their peers or the European Commission or a host of critical academics.

From 2005/2006 co-ordination between Member States improved and implementation gained momentum. The goal of "becoming the most competitive economy in the world by the year 2010", as it was formulated, too, in 2000, may have been too ambitious, and beyond reach for the time being, but the European economy today seems in better shape and long-term perspectives seem better than has been the case for many years. Let me stress that I am talking long-term here and structural developments, not the possibility of a temporary economic downturn following the bubble–and–downturn in the US. The Lisbon Agenda is mostly about micro-economic issues — education, research and development, competition and the business climate — but at the same time the EU economies have taken great strides to improve macro-economic performance and stability.

In the 1990's, after the inflation and stagflation years of the 1980's, many EU Member States struggled with government deficits and debts. The years 1992 and 1993 saw two serious crises during the EU's effort to maintain fixed exchange rates among participating states. It took considerable time and effort (and spending) from Europe's biggest Member State Germany, to manage the economic fallout of the reunification of East and West Germany, not least of the politically probably inevitable, but economically difficult decision to fix the exchange rate of the currencies of East and West at one-to-one. The strains were heavy and the pains were considerable. The European Commission's economic analysis department (now the Directorate General for Economic and Financial Affairs, DG ECFIN) in its "Country Study, Germany" of 2004 expressed serious concerns about Germany's long-term outlook and not least competitiveness with ever rising wage costs and unemployment and increasing budget deficits and government debt.[57]

At the same time, Germany's condition for accepting the launch of the euro was that possibly "less responsible Member States" would be disciplined through the "Stability and Growth Pact". This was an agreement that put the "Maastricht criteria" even more fixed in stone: thou shalt not have a government deficit of more than 3 percent, thou shalt not have a government debt of more than 60 percent. The Pact ruled that Member States who breached the deficit requirement would be under scrutiny and might even be fined. Only several years later, in the first years after the coming to birth of the euro, it was Germany itself which had great difficulty to stick to the rules and finally had to admit that for a while it couldn't. The pardon Germany and also France finally received instead of the humiliation of having to pay a financial penalty, led some voters in smaller Member States to conclude that "as always the Big Boys call the shots and can get away with it". It helped develop an anti-euro mood and anti-EU mood in considerable parts of the EU.[58] In Germany the euro was referred to as "teuro", "teuer" meaning expensive. In 2005, in the Netherlands the radical left "Socialist Party"(the party has Stalinist roots and is governed in authoritarian style) successfully campaigned against the adoption of the EU constitution by Dutch voters with the lie "you know, too, that prices have doubled because of the euro".

---

[57] European Commission, Country Study Germany, 1994.

[58] It did contribute to the new anti-EU mood in the Netherlands which led to the Dutch no-vote in the EU constitution referendum in 2005 (it was the only national referendum ever held in the Netherlands).

However, such hesitations, criticism and anti-feelings notwithstanding and even if we consider that the ten-year old euro is still too young to allow us to decide to what extent is a success, it would be difficult *not* to conclude that the more cautious fiscal and monetary policy course chosen by the EU is paying off. I made the point that after years of struggling with ever rising government debts EU governments are now seeking to outdo each other with balanced budgets and surpluses even. The European Central Bank's (ECB) policy has more than once been qualified as overly conservative. It has in particular been criticised for being too much focused on fighting inflation and not caring enough about economic growth. For the time being, however, that policy, conservative or not, seems to have served the EU economy well and probably the world economy too. Greater caution in fiscal and monetary policy in the EU and in particular in the euro area has no doubt contributed to greater stability today and possibly to greater long-term growth potential in the EU too.[59]

So the EU decided to adhere to the EU Lisbon Agenda (which stands, as I put it in my shorthand for: *greater macro-economic stability and government action to help markets function better*) and to improve macro-economic stability. It is ironic that practically at the same time in the US a new republican administration took the helm that chose an almost opposite course: a micro-economic market–knows–best and hands–off attitude, an overly lax fiscal policy and an extremely loose, if not reckless, monetary policy.

I pointed at the big difference between the bilateral trade deficit the US has with China and the one the EU has. The US has a large *overall* current account deficit, of close to 5 percent of GDP (2007/2008), whereas the EU's overall current account is practically in balance. In the US, the economic policy choice has deliberately been for a lax fiscal regime (tax cuts combined with higher expenditure) which has resulted in a rapidly rising government debt. Monetary policy has

---

[59] To compare, once again, with the US, under the present circumstances no EU Member State could afford (or would be "allowed") to build up government debt at a speed the US government is doing at the moment.

been particularly loose with periods of considerable length when real (short-term) interest rates, set by monetary policy planners, were negative. This policy approach may have contributed to the high current account deficit and the continuous fall of the dollar. Recent Federal Reserve Board decisions seem not only to confirm, but even to acerbate the policies of the previous Federal Reserve Board chairman. America's lax monetary policy course can even be mentioned as a possibly likely factor to explain the surge in worldwide inflation that began in early 2008.

As for market regulation, unwillingness by the Federal Reserve Board to strengthen financial oversight when warnings about excesses and outright fraud in the US mortgage market began to emerge may have helped the mortgage debacle emerge in the US. Today, following this US made storm there is renewed consensus in the US that greater regulation of US financial markets is needed. The lack of regulation of US financial markets is taking its toll, not least on US taxpayers who have to pick up part of the bill. This bill is among other things going to be paid through US government coverage of Government Sponsored Enterprise (GSE) Fannie Mae, and Freddie Mac whose debt was USD 800 billion, 6 percent of US GDP, in early 2008. The contradiction of the US version of capitalism is that what is presented as the ultimate example of unfettered capitalism has a considerable potential of tax-financed security-cushions built in for *investors* or *lenders* ("capitalists") who got it wrong. The built-in cushions of the EU economy come under the name "social security" and are mostly designed to protect *labour* against shocks, rather than capital. The signs are that today's turmoil may lead to a new swing of the pendulum in the US back to greater regulation and government intervention in markets (and by implication bringing its system somewhat closer to the "EU model").

It seems plausible that following the marked differences in the macro-economic policy course taken on each side of the Atlantic, the EU economy today, unlike 10 or 15 years ago, is more shock-proof than the US one and better capable to face the challenge from China (and India and other emerging economies in Asia). The EU macro-economic environment has further been helped by the enlargements in 2004 and 2007,[60] which has led to greater dynamism through increased trade, investment, including cross-border investment, and labour migration. In particular intra-EU labour migration was met with opposition immediately after the enlargement of 2004 and most "old" Member States only gradually allowed labour from the new Member States in, but the transition which is still going on, has led to fewer disruptions than expected and this fact has led to gradually growing acceptance.

With regard to Europe's North/South divide, macro-economic indicators show that Italy, Greece and Portugal are struggling with at least several of the following macro-economic ills: high government debt (still above 100 percent of GDP in Italy) and deficits, macro-economic competitiveness (cost/price) problems and current account deficits. One cannot escape from the impression that these three countries have difficulty to cope with the economic discipline implied by the euro. Of the Southern European countries Spain has for a long time been the success story. Thanks to the euro and euro-inspired domestic economic policy Spain managed to reduce its government debt and to attract substantial flows of foreign investment. However, the country was also the first to suffer serious trouble from the economic headwinds that began to blow in 2008. Only time can tell if Spain's current recession will be short-lived and if it will thrive again afterwards.

II.5.2. *The More Inclusive EU: Social Security*

There is no need here to elaborate into great detail the argument that Europe, the EU, has a much wider and thorough social safety net than the US. The evidence is abundant and in particular the disadvantages of this European Social Model (ESM) have been elaborated on extensively, in particular, in the 1980's and 1990's, when the costs appeared to be too heavy a burden on European economies to stay

---

[60] 10 new Member States in 2004, 8 of which were former communist countries (Czech Republic, Estonia, Hungary, Latria, Lithuania, Poland, Slovenia, Slovakia) and another two, also formerly communist, Bulgaria and Romania in 2007.

competitive. Under the pressure of the economic convergence and prudence that was required by the introduction of the Maastricht budget criteria, government budgets, including social security and unemployment systems[61] have, however, improved and so has expenditure control. Europe's extensive social security system has been trimmed somewhat in the last 15 years although it is still very generous by international standards[62] and probably too costly.

The signs are, however, that for the moment the costs are politically accepted. Population ageing seems the biggest challenge ahead. First concerned are pensions systems where none of the Southern EU Member States has a funded system. The second major challenge concerns health care systems which show a great variety of access, coverage and financing among Member States. Only the UK has a fully state-run "national health system", in all other EU Member States market forces play to varying degrees a role in the health care system. It is, once again comparing the EU and the US, striking that the US is the only high-income country without a national health insurance.

Thirdly, with unemployment in the Euro-zone at a low (although still 7 percent and not likely to go further down soon — edging up rather) the costs for unemployment systems seem at least to have become bearable, in particular because *employment* rates among the population are still on the rise in most EU Member States although there are large differences between countries.

In particular in the Nordic countries in Europe and more recently the Netherlands too, have been successful in maintaining a high degree of social security and equality together with a modest level of unemployment, which keeps funding sustainable. This has in particular in Sweden, Finland, Denmark and the Netherlands been achieved by a more active policy of putting pressure on beneficiaries of working age

---

[61] "Government revenue" refers to all "taxes" including mandatory social security contributions. It is useful to keep this in mind when comparing "taxation rates" (as percent of GDP) between countries. In some EU countries taxes in the strict sense are not much higher than in other OECD countries; costs for the social security system (which may include health care) form the major difference.

[62] On the other hand, website www.wsws.org reports for the US "food stamp use projected to swell to record levels", a figure of "more than 10 percent of US households" is mentioned.

to participate in the labour market. Anthony Giddens in his "Europe in the Global Age" makes the point that these achievements "come not from *refusing* reform, but from *embracing* it".[63] These same four countries have also sustainable, funded pension systems. Germany, France and Italy, on the other hand, are examples of countries where pressure on unemployed to return to the labour market is much less whereas (or possibly precisely because of this fact) some two thirds of unemployment in the EU is in these three countries where labour market policy can best be characterised as *protecting jobs* rather than *workers.*

Europe's unemployment schemes, although trimmed, remain generous by international standards, which will without doubt contribute to a greater feeling of security among the European labour force with regard to competition form outside the EU. Both attitude vis-à-vis wages and social welfare systems in place have led to a Gini inequality coefficient of 31 percent in the EU, even after the EU took 12 considerably poorer countries on board, against 45 percent in the US. It seems reasonable to assume that all these factors together contribute to the EU to be a more "inclusive society" than the US where with an unemployment rate of 5.1 percent (considerably lower than in Europe) 10 percent of households is on food stamps (welfare, not "earned" social security one is "entitled" too).

II.5.3. *The More Inclusive EU: Education*

Also education and access to education are, it seems, in the EU, more equally distributed among the population than is the case in the US. International comparisons indicate that top education in the US is without doubt world top. According to a ranking by the Shanghai Jiao Tong University, American universities make up 8 of the top 10 universities of the world and 44 of the top 50. Some institutions in other parts of the world, including in Europe are gradually catching up, but until today there is, for instance, a net flow from top European researchers to the US. At the same time, however, Europe and other high-income economies in the world are better and broader

---

[63] Anthony Giddens, *Europe in the Global Age*, 2007.

at the "sub–top", in particular in secondary education. In most European countries access to secondary and university education of average and of good quality is free or available at prices far below prices in the US for education of more than average quality. The above finds support from international comparisons. The largest and widest comparative survey of overall country–wide educational performance is the valuable OECD's (Organisation for Economic Cooperation and Development) Programme for International Student Assessment (PISA).

The PISA survey is held every three years. The last time was in 2006 when it was held among 400,000 15-year olds in 57 countries (OECD member states and in a variety of non-member countries throughout the world). Skills and knowledge tested in 2006 relate to the areas of science, reading and mathematics, "essential for full participation in society" as OECD/PISA puts it[64] and meeting the demands of the labour market of today's rapidly developing economies. Finland was the highest scoring country/economy on the PISA 2006 scale. Other good scores were obtained by Canada, Japan, New Zealand, Hong Kong, Taiwan, Estonia, Australia, the Netherlands, Korea, Germany, the UK, the Czech Republic, Switzerland, Austria, Belgium and Ireland. At the bottom were Azerbaijan, Kyrgyzstan, Tunisia, Brazil and Argentina.

The relatively low scores of the US tests are not only surprising, if not striking, because of the US's high income per head, but also because of her reputation for excellence in education. This excellence apparently is limited, however, to institutions at the top of the scale and possibly to tertiary education (university level) more in general. But access to secondary education of reasonable quality is unevenly distributed, because quality comes at a considerable price. Secondary education is precisely the minimum level of education required for properly performing many of today's so-called blue collar jobs in manufacturing. In the PISA test results of 57 countries the US's average score is 29th in the science test and 33rd in the mathematics.

---

[64] All data are from the OECD/PISA website www.pisa.oecd.org, which is a rich source of information.

OECD/PISA, scores of 15-year-olds, maximum = 600, EU and US (out of 57 participating countries); last column "average" is my calculation (the sum of both scores divided by two)

Rank	From best to worst average	Science	Mathematics	Average Science and Mathematics
1	Finland	563	548	555
2	Netherlands	525	531	528
3	Estonia	531	515	523
4	Belgium	510	520	515
5	Slovenia	519	504	511
6	Czech Republic	512	510	511
7	Germany	516	504	510
8	Austria	511	505	508
9	UK	515	495	505
10/11	Denmark	496	513	504
10/11	Ireland	508	501	504
12	Sweden	503	502	502
13	Hungary	504	491	497
14	Poland	498	495	496
15	France	495	496	495
16	Slovakia	488	492	490
17/18	Latvia	490	486	488
17/18	Luxembourg	486	490	488
19	Lithuania	488	486	487
20	Spain	488	480	484
21	**United States**	**489**	**474**	**482**
22	Portugal	474	466	470
23	Italy	475	462	468
24	Greece	473	459	466
25	Bulgaria	434	413	423
26	Romania	418	415	416

The most obvious conclusion is that like income, education and access to education, in particular secondary education, are in the US less evenly distributed than in most other rich nations. This also implies that the US is more than the EU likely to have a major problem with cases like Mr. Middleton whom we met in Section II.3 and who had always wanted to do "the same thing" his father did in the steel mill.

The low average score among 15-year-old Americans leads me to conclude that too many young Americans are poorly educated by the minimum standards of an advanced economy. Just as Mr. Middleton, who was introduced above, they may have difficulty to meet the requirements of the labour market of a developed economy today, even when it concerns "blue collar" manufacturing jobs. The question is not so much if someone from China or India (or Mexico) is now doing Mr. Middleton's job ("stole" it). The question is rather if Mr. Middleton and others at the lower end of the "skills scale" have the skills to find a proper job where they can be productive and add value and, consequently, command a decent salary. Such a job would in general require well developed reading and writing skills and the ability to understand abstract schemes and diagrams. It would not very likely be "the thing my father and both my grandfathers always did", but it would seem entirely off the point and unfair to blame China for that. David Brooks in a piece in the US newspaper the "International Herald Tribune" stressed the need that we should be aware of the requirements of what he refers to as the cognitive age.[65] At the end of his article he refers to the context of the democratic/republican divide in the US, which I refer to as the left/right divide:

> The globalization paradigm leads people to see economic development as a form of foreign policy, as a grand competition between nations and civilizations. These abstractions, called "the Chinese" or "the Indians" are doing this or that. But the cognitive age paradigm emphasizes psychology, culture and pedagogy — the specific processes that foster learning. It emphasizes that different societies are being stressed in similar ways by increased demands on human capital. If you understand that you are living in the cognitive age, you're focusing on the real source of prosperity and understand that your anxiety is not being caused by a foreigner. It's not that globalization and the skills revolution are contradictory processes.

---

[65] David Brooks, *The Cognitive Age*, International Herald Tribune, 3-4 May, 2008.

But which paradigm you embrace determines which facts and remedies you emphasize. Politicians, especially Democratic ones, have fallen in love with the globalization paradigm. It's time to move beyond it.

It is interesting to pursue the North/South question in the EU, and I am inclined to consider it as more than pure coincidence, that in the table above, which summarises PISA outcomes for EU Member States and the US, EU Member States that come after the US are "Southern" Italy, Greece and Portugal, followed only by Bulgaria and Romania. The table shows the average test scores for science and mathematics (plus the averages of these two as I calculated them) on a scale from zero to 600 for 25 EU Member States (no test scores for Cyprus and Malta are available) and the US, ranked from top to bottom. The score for reading for the US was missing in the tables on the OECD/PISA website and I therefore left the reading scores out altogether, also for the EU. In general reading scores for EU Member States don't differ very much from the scores for science and mathematics so for the EU countries in the table, the average scores would not have been very different had I included them.

II.5.4. *World Bank Indicators of Good Governance, EU and US Compared*

In the table below I summarise scores of the World Bank good governance indicators[66] for 20 EU Member States, once again compared with the US. The government indicator figures are rankings (percentile data) based on subjective judgements and interesting as they may be, these indicators should be seen as giving no more than indeed an indication. It is nevertheless noticeable how similar the country ranking for "governance" is to the much more objective OECD/PISA skills–and–knowledge–performance tests of 15-year-olds

---

[66] A rich set of data, accessible through http://info.worldbank.org/governance/wgi2007/sc_country.asp.

in the previous section. Northern EU Member States lead the ranking and once again scores for the US are just ahead of those for France, Portugal, Greece, Spain and Italy.

The statistical evidence is less straightforward here than in the case of the PISA scores. The PISA scores are, moreover, precisely measured fairly "hard" data whereas the governance indicator data are percentile rankings based on opinions expressed and therefore much "softer". We further should note that the differences between the governance indicators for the various countries are not very large and it may therefore very well be argued that caution should be taken with drawing conclusions from these data.

These caveats notwithstanding, it is tempting to point at the fact that, once again, the US is also in this comparison in one pack with the more Southern EU Member States. However, to weaken the case for making firm conclusions, among the poorer performers there are a number of new EU Member States as well who are not particularly known for their anti-free trade position in the EU Council of Ministers. A plausible counter-explanation for this seemingly contradictory finding is that these new Member States, cultural and historical considerations aside, haven't adopted the euro yet and hence still have the flexibility offered by a more independent monetary policy, most of all exchange rate policy. Italy, in particular, was for decades used to "competitive devaluations". It is clear that today this country has great difficulty in coping with the requirements and the discipline of the euro, not only in the area of trade, but also in their overall managing of costs and prices in its economy. It is not without reason that some analysts suggest that Italy may have to abandon the euro one day.

In the context of the governance indicators it would be tempting to point as well at government policies with regard to business regulation, competition,[67] the rule of law and, above all, education.

---

[67] The latest bizarre episode in Italy's economic management unfolded in March and April, 2008, when an attempt by Air France/KLM to buy ailing Alitalia was first blocked by Alitalia's unions and subsequently by the newly elected Italian government — which instead pumped budget money in the company.

However, given the caveats, I leave the question open whether one may conclude from the results shown above that the problems of the US and Southern EU Member States in the context of the "China threat", competition from low-wage countries in general and the technology challenge, are rooted in basic conditions which are related and which these countries have in common. I leave it to the reader to decide whether the results of the test presented in this section are convincing enough.

The results of the PISA education test, however, seem sufficiently convincing. With regard to education greater access in the US and better adjustment to the requirements of the labour market both in the US and Southern EU Member States seem to be key issues to address when it comes to the question of how to deal with the challenge of globalisation and competition from low-wage countries.

To conclude, the tentative findings of Section II.5 are the following:

• Concerns about China and free trade are in the US mostly a left/right issue whereas in the EU opinions are split along a South/North line rather.

• Possible explanations for this difference are that in the EU in comparison with the US — and in the Northern Member States more markedly than in the Southern ones — there is greater macro-economic stability, better social security and better overall, average access to secondary education of reasonable quality.

II.5.5. *But ... Is This Analysis Correct?*

It is time for a short timeout. After the analysis above I have started wondering about my own findings. Is the US not the most vital and dynamic economy on earth with greater underlying strength than any other economy? In the 1990's, I worked for a few years as an analyst of the German economy. The conclusion we came to at the

World Bank indicators of good governance (from: World Bank, Kaufmann & Kraay), percentiles; EU Member States compared with US; note how close this ranking comes to the OECD/PISA ranking

Rank (average)	Democracy voice & account.	Stability	Government effective?	Regulatory quality	Rule of law	Anti corruption policy	Average. Not weighted
1 FI[68]	98	100	98	97	98	100	98
2/3 DK	100	75	100	100	100	100	95
2/3 SW	97	88	97	93	97	97	95
4 AUS	96	82	92	95	97	95	93
5 NL	99	71	95	95	94	96	93
6 DE	95	75	91	91	94	94	92
7 UK	93	60	95	98	93	94	90
8 Belgium	95	69	92	88	91	91	89
9/10 US	84	58	93	94	92	89	85
9/10 PT	90	76	90	87	83	83	85
11 France	92	62	86	83	90	92	84
12 Slovn.	85	83	85	73	75	81	80
13 Spain	80	60	82	82	85	84	79
14 Hung.	87	67	73	86	74	70	76
15/16 Slovk.	78	76	78	83	61	66	74
15/16 CZ R	77	70	80	80	73	66	74
17 Greece	80	63	80	73	68	72	73
18 Italy	86	56	67	74	60	64	68
19 Poland	77	54	70	70	60	60	65
20 Bulg.	65	63	64	68	53	54	61
21 Rom.	62	57	54	55	48	45	54

68 AUS = Austria; Bulg. = Bulgaria; CZ R = Czech Republic; DE = Germany; DK = Denmark; FI = Finland; Hung. = Hungary; NL = Netherlands; PT = Portugal; Rom. = Romania; Slovk. = Slovakia; Slovn. = Slovenia; SW = Sweden.

time was very different from my conclusions above: the German economy was in serious long-term trouble, lagging behind in productivity, innovation and other measures of performance when compared with the US.[69] Have things changed so significantly in the 15 years that passed? Has Europe done so well since then and has US policy so seriously failed its people?

To add to my doubts, in early June 2008 the US Rand Corporation published a study which stresses America's competitive edge in no uncertain terms[70]:

> Is the United States in danger of losing its competitive edge in science and technology (S&T)? This concern has been raised repeatedly since the end of the Cold War, most recently in a wave of reports in the mid-2000s suggesting that globalization and the growing strength of other nations in S&T, coupled with inadequate US investments in research and education, threaten the United States' position of leadership in S&T. Galama and Hosek examine these claims and contrast them with relevant data, including trends in research and development investment; information on the size, composition, and pay of the US science and engineering workforce; and domestic and international education statistics. They find that the United States continues to lead the world in science and technology and has kept pace or grown faster than other nations on several measurements of S&T performance; that it generally benefits from the influx of foreign S&T students and workers; and that the United States will continue to benefit from the development of new technologies by other nations as long as it maintains the capability to acquire and implement such technologies. However, US leadership in science and technology must not be taken for granted, and Galama and Hosek conclude with recommendations to strengthen the US S&T enterprise, including measures to facilitate the immigration of highly skilled labor and improve the US education system.

---

[69] European Commission, Country Study Germany, 1994.
[70] www.rand.org/pubs/monographs/MG674, June 2008.

The analysis by the Rand Corporation is, however, not necessarily contradicting my assessment, which is that at the top of the knowledge ladder the US continues to be top ("S&T"), but that America's problem concerns the sub-top and below rather. Along with its optimism the Rand Corporation study stresses the need to "improve the US education system." My assessment is that especially in the area of secondary education in the US major improvement and particularly better access to quality is needed. The US should ensure much wider access to secondary education of decent quality. This particular question is not addressed in the Rand Corporation study, but I argue, that this would improve the way in which America's lower middle class or "blue collar workers" will be able to cope with foreign competition.

The point I make above is that Europe through its more "inclusive approach" might be in a better position to let the lower middle class cope with challenges posed by China, India and globalisation in general. First, in Europe access to secondary education of acceptable quality is better and more affordable than in the US, leading to better average scores in the OECD/PISA tests, which, I assume, reflects greater capacity to adapt of the lower skilled labour force. And second, Europe's social security safety net is a positive factor. Europe's social security has its costs and certainly leads to abuse too, but the US system seems to lead to a greater number of outcasts (food stamps and worse).

Can one really claim or assume, as I tend to do, that Europe may be in a better position than the US to withstand global competition? And suppose it is indeed the case today, how sustainable is this advantage? In May 2008, protests in Asia against rising prices of food and fuel (the latter after the abolition of subsidies) were followed by protests in Europe, especially against rising fuel prices. In Europe the protests were first organised by European truckers and fishermen. The latter, after depleting practically nearby seas of fish, have to sail ever further to find a proper catch, which means using ever more fuel to get to their fishing grounds. Later on civil servants and other groups joined or organised demonstrations of their own. These protests were against rising prices in general and national governments or "Brussels" (the EU) were asked to take measures.

China and globalisation were not mentioned by the protesters in Europe. Even oil exporting countries were not accused. The culprits were national governments and "Brussels" or "the EU". We may have to conclude that angry Europeans don't blame globalisation for their suffering, but their governments or "capitalists". Perhaps the simple explanation is that Europeans don't know very well how the mechanisms of world markets work in an age of global capitalism. Perhaps it is Europeans' reflex to turn to their governments when they are in need. Looking at Germany again, it is surprising to see how "old fashioned" the wishes of the emerging "new" Left party there (Die Linke) are. It is all "back to the sixties": profit is a dirty word, workers are exploited, wages should be increased and so should social benefits, and the government budget is limitless, it seems.

China, globalisation, international competition or budget constraints don't seem to exist for the German Left ("Die Linke") or other radical left parties. With elections on the horizon the present German coalition government of centre right Christian Democrats and centre left Social Democrats has reversed and is further reversing a number of reforms, decided by the previous government of Social Democrats, which meant to improve (and did improve) Germany's competitiveness. Perhaps in a few years from now the tables are turned again and the gains of the last few years squandered. Only time can tell.

Let me put in a second caveat. It should be kept in mind that part of the analysis in the previous sub-chapters is about perceptions and opinions, which may change quickly, depending on events. As we saw perceptions of China in Europe changed considerably between June 2007 and March/April 2008. The most plausible explanation for this change is the extensive media coverage of protests in Tibet and the Chinese response, and events surrounding the Olympic torch relay, both events in March and early April 2008. Both events apparently, and understandably, have their impact on "China perceptions" whereas while reflecting a certain situation and reminding the public of that situation, these events do not in themselves change the EU-China relationship. In spite of the caveats, it seems, and I believe, that for the time being a plausible case can be made that in Europe, with the exception of the Southern Member States, and more in particular, Italy, there is less "China fear" and "globalisation fear" than in the US.

Chapter III

The Real Challenge, the Environment: The Return of Malthus?

III.1. Environmental Consequences of China's Rise

The real challenge of the rise of China (and India and Asia in general) lies in the environmental implications, much more so than today's trade questions and concerns about jobs and wages in rich countries. The latter are, as I have argued above, often overblown and if not there is not much the West can do other than to cope with them and improve its own competitiveness. The environmental implications, on the other hand, are huge, because it is about large countries, which see sudden and high economic growth. All figures on the matter are staggering, once again and above all, because of the numbers involved. China's population today is 1.3 billion. When we add India's 1.1 billion and ASEAN's 500 million, we get at total of 2.9 billion or 44 percent of the world population. In this section I will focus on the situation in China. In the next section I will elaborate on the more worldwide perspective. However, given China's size and, in addition, the pollution already caused by today's rich countries it all comes down to this one question: is this sustainable?

For China alone the catalogue of examples is long enough. The arithmetic is straightforward and the results are scaring. Today China has 30 million private automobiles, a little more than two cars for every 100 persons; vehicle sales are 500,000 each month and on a rising trend. By 2020 China is expected to have 130 million cars. If say in 2050, China with a population of 1.4 billion, were to have a car density similar to the EU's (450 cars per 1000 population) there would be something like 600 million cars on China's roads, more than double the number of cars on US roads today (where car density is 800 cars per 1,000 population). The launch, in January 2008, of the Nano — the Indian Tata Group's "people's car" which will be for sale for USD 2500 — makes this scenario only more likely.

Let us take another example: the capacity *added* to China's power grid *each year* is approximately equal to the UK's *total* power capacity. In spite of considerable expansion of China's nuclear capacity coal is to remain the country's main source of electricity production for a long time to come. So consequently and inevitably and in spite of Chinese efforts to curb emissions, China's *additional* emissions each year for electricity generation alone are at least the equivalent of the UK's emissions for power generation today (possibly more). Suppose that the UK manages to reduce its annual emissions for electricity generation by 20 percent or 30 percent in 2020. In the meantime China will have added 12 to 13 times today's UK emissions to the world's total emissions, perhaps "only" 10 times that amount if China too were to manage to reduce its emissions relative to the amount of power generation by 20 percent or 30 percent. Emissions by industry and road and air transport are not included in this example. We should keep in mind that even the most ambitious efforts to curb the annual flow of emissions in the Kyoto context, welcome as they may be, are all about *reducing the extra*. They are about *adding less*, not about the stock of greenhouse gases already out there, mostly produced by today's rich countries in the last two centuries.

An area where very important gains can be made is energy efficiency, energy consumption in proportion to GDP growth. It is also called energy productivity, as we speak of labour and capital productivity. Like other countries China is already constantly improving its energy efficiency. This is from a very low efficiency, highly polluting base however. Once again, given China's mere size and its high rate of economic growth, it would seem inevitable that China, and therefore the world, is faced with continuously rising demand for energy and a continuous rise of related emissions for many years to come whatever measures are taken.

"Though China has made great strides to improve the energy efficiency of its industrial base over the past 20 years, statistics show there is still a long way to go. Heating, lighting, and cooling public buildings alone accounts for five percent of China's energy consumption. Per ton of steel produced a Chinese steel maker uses three times more energy than a Japanese steel maker. On average China's key energy-consuming industries use anywhere from 12 to 98 percent more energy per unit of production than those in developed countries."[71] The silver lining is that this points at a huge potential for improvement and gains. With oil above 100 US dollar per barrel (125 US dollar per barrel in May 2008 and rising) prospects for energy saving investments change drastically.

In China, like in many Asian countries, electricity and oil are subsidised. As in the past in Europe, this makes the sales price of electricity lower than its production costs. Electricity is considered as a sort of "public" good and governments seek to reduce costs and improve competitiveness of companies. In May 2008, facing ever higher oil prices and consequently, rising costs of these subsidies for their budgets, a number of Asian governments had to reduce subsidies or abolish them altogether. Petrol prices went up 11 percent in India, 30 percent in Indonesia and 41 percent in Malaysia. It remains to be seen what the social and political repercussions are. China's budget situation was comfortable enough to maintain subsidies for a while, but shortly afterwards Chinese subsidies were also reduced. Subsidies obviously do not help to promote a more efficient use of energy. Given the potential size of China's demand for oil, subsidies in China help keep Chinese demand high and consequently world oil prices. Once subsidies can be phased out entirely as Asian countries become richer, energy saving measures will become more attractive.

In its 11th five-year plan of March 2006, the Chinese government announced that it wanted to improve energy efficiency (productivity) by 4 percent per year in the five year period of the plan. This objective

---

[71] Pam Baldinger, *Lean and Green: Boosting Chinese Energy Efficiency through ESCOs*, Worldbank, China Environment Series, Issue 5.

was not very ambitious — China was already on a path of an improvement of energy efficiency of 3 percent per year — and still the objective was not met in the first two years of implementation. Nevertheless, if the objective of 4 percent annual efficiency gain is achieved over a period of 12 years, i.e., until 2020, China's energy use would be 60 percent of what it would have been otherwise. If we assume a doubling of GDP over the same period, although on current trends GDP would grow by a lot more than this 100 percent, China's energy consumption could be "only" 20 percent above today's level. Provided that better technology is developed emissions could perhaps be lower than today's.

McKinsey's Global Institute (MGI) projects considerable potential gains from greater energy efficiency in China (and the US for that matter) provided that the right investments are made in existing techniques. MGI estimates that with an investment 1 percent of its present total annual investment China could by 2020 have lowered its energy/GDP ratio by 23 percent, oil imports by 15 percent and carbon dioxide emissions by 20 percent.[72] This is in fact a less optimistic scenario than the one above based on the 4 percent gain per year.

Policy efforts and improvements notwithstanding, China has huge environmental problems, part of which it exports in the form of polluted water and greenhouse gases. In an article in Foreign Affairs Elizabeth Economy (EE) presents a long list of China's woes.[73] Among them: the country's use of coal for 70 percent of its primary energy needs and huge energy inefficiencies (for the production of 1 euro of GDP China needs seven times more energy than Japan and four times more than the world average); the rapidly rising use of refrigerators, air-conditioners and dishwashers; deforestation; widespread water pollution (700 million people would drink water contaminated with animal and human waste; EE speaks of a "plundering of ground-water reserves"). China has cracked down on domestic logging, but has become the world's largest importer of illegally logged timber instead. It is tempting to quote more from EE's stark language and many examples. None of them are new, but put

---

[72] www.mckinsey.com/mgi/publications/curbing_Energy/Index.asp
[73] Elizabeth Economy, *The Great Leap Backward?*, Foreign Affairs, September/October 2007.

together and listed in staccato style they are very effective in giving a worrying picture:

> As China's pollution woes increase so, too, do the risks to its economy, public health, social stability, and international reputation. As Pan Yue, the Vice Minister of China's State Environmental Protection Agency (SEPA), warned in 2005: "The economic miracle will end soon because the environment can no longer keep pace" (…) China's rapid development, often touted as an economic miracle, has become an environmental disaster. Record growth necessarily requires gargantuan consumption resources, but in China energy use has been especially unclean and inefficient, with dire consequences for the country's air, land and water.

There are estimates that the cost of environmental degradation and resource depletion in China may have been of the order of at least 5 percent of China's GDP each year and possibly more. This would mean that "real" or "true" or sustainable economic growth is considerably lower than the well-known "headline" figure for economic growth of 10 percent per year. In 2004, Chinese leaders announced that a new green GDP would replace the Chinese standard GDP. Actively obstructed by the Chinese National Bureau for Statistics the effort was shelved when it became clear that the adjustment for environmental damage would reduce economic growth to politically unacceptable levels. Environmental damage and resource depletion appeared to be far more prevalent and costly than anticipated.[74]

China's political leadership has shown that it is well aware of the problem, but, like political leaders in any economy, it has to find a politically acceptable balance between the need to continue delivering material goods and meet standard GDP growth measures today while at the same time addressing environmental problems. It concerns the standard choice that has to be made, also in other countries, between produced goods today and the more long-term costs of environmental

---

[74] An interesting side effect of this failed attempt is that a search of "Green GDP" in GOOGLE produces many references to China.

destruction in the process. There is, in addition, an implementation problem which is more specific for China and other decentralised nations in general (China is a much more decentralised country than it is often assumed).

As it is the case with other Chinese laws and rules, decisions taken and policies pursued by Beijing risk being nullified by local authorities. These local authorities are often more keen to achieve standard GDP targets than environmental ones and more interested in accomplishing brick-and-mortar and concrete-and-steel projects in their region than "saving the environment". Very often local authorities are operating like little (or big) entrepreneurs who want to achieve their "targets" without the hassle of "soft" environmental targets. And, as the Chinese saying goes, "the mountain is high and the emperor is far away".

Ironically, in the US, another example of a decentralised nation, albeit a much richer one, the opposite is happening. Faced with Washington's unwillingness to follow a more responsible environmental policy course, individual US states and cities have begun to apply environmental measures of their own, with California as the best known example. With regard to China and on a more optimistic note one may point out that the backing from local authorities of more environment friendly policies depends on creating the right incentives for these authorities. Among such incentives greater responsiveness towards environmental concerns of the population could play a more prominent role one day.

Together with income inequality, rising inflation and corruption, large-scale pollution forms arguably one of the most serious threats to social stability, China's international reputation and the legitimacy of the role of the Communist Party. Environmental problems have led to riots and demonstrations. The central government is gradually tolerating the work of environmental NGOs to operate, albeit somewhat half-heartedly and within strict limits as environmental campaigner Wu Lihong learned the hard way. For 16 years Wu campaigned against pollution in Tai Hu and was in 2005 honoured for his efforts by Beijing, only to be jailed later by local authorities on dubious charges of blackmail.

A fairly optimistic view of China's situation and perspectives is presented by J.M. Dean and M.E. Lovely in a thorough paper in which they focus on the relationship between China's pollution and its trade.[75] According to their data "industrial pollution intensity has already stabilized and, in many industries, has begun to decline". They argue that in particular China's export industry has become considerably less polluting in the last decade because of technological improvements and the changing character of China's exports.

Exports have increasingly shifted to final assembly as the result of what the authors refer to as "fragmentation". In principle this is good news, of course, but one has to consider that even if the pollution *intensity* of exports stabilises or declines, overall pollution (related to exports) is still increasing considerably when trade continues growing by more than 20 percent per year. On the other hand, we cannot exclude that energy efficiency improvement is accelerated and the MGI projections I mentioned above and which sketch a scenario of a decrease in China's overall energy demand and emissions, are realized.

It seems worthwhile to quote what Dean and Lovely write about the government's continuous effort to address environmental problems:

> The Chinese government has long recognized the need for environmental protection. In 1989 a legislative base for environment protection was created by promulgation of the Environmental Protection Law. (...) the State Environmental Protection Agency (SEPA) was given ministerial rank in 1998 (...). In each province, 6 Environmental Protection Bureaus oversee compliance with national and local environmental regulations. These local Bureaus report to provincial administrators, which also oversee their funding. Recently, SEPA has acquired some say in the selection of provincial EPB heads. EPBs also exist at the prefecture or municipal, and district or county levels. EPBs report directly to upper level environmental administrators as well as to the government of a geographic

---

[75] J.M. Dean, M.E. Lovely, *Trade Growth, Production Fragmentation, and China's Environment*, NBER, March 2008.

area. This reporting system is often cited as a source of conflict for local EPBs who may face interference from local leaders. (...) China has a well-developed regulatory system with over 2,000 laws related to environmental protection. During the 1990s, China gave increasing emphasis to prevention and shifted responsibility to polluters to pay for environmental damage.

And to add to the above: at the National Party Congress, in March 2008, the status of the SEPA was further upgraded. China has become more open about its environmental problems. The degree of pollution seems to be decreasing now, which doesn't mean, however, that pollution is not continuing, let alone that the environmental situation is improving. So what is the conclusion? Is the glass half-full or half-empty? Much damage has been done and is still being done to the environment in China, but serious efforts for improvement are being made. Much, very much, remains to be done, however, and China's economic growth is high and continues rising at great speed. Consequently, in spite of the efforts to reduce emissions and to improve energy efficiency, in 2008 China bypassed the USA as the biggest emitter of greenhouse gasses on earth.

Given the difference in population size this means that emissions per Chinese are still no more than 23 percent of emissions per American. On current trends, the US will remain the biggest polluter per person for a long time to come. Taking into account the difference in the level of income between the US and China, it appears that China produces 38 percent more carbon dioxide per dollar of GDP than the US (GDP at PPP, i.e., measured as the volume of goods). But the US, the richest nation on earth, is not a very good yardstick. GDP (at PPP) per head in the US is 40 percent higher than in the EU, but the US produces 150 percent more carbon dioxide emissions per head.[76] These figures would mean that *the production of one dollar of US GDP leads to 78 percent more carbon dioxide emissions than the production of one dollar of EU GDP; the production*

---

[76] *UNDP Human Development Report*, 2007/2008, see table with emissions per head further in this text.

of one dollar of Chinese GDP to 146 percent more emissions. There is still a long way to go, a very long one, because also the EU, although it does better than the US and China, has to reduce its emissions.

The EU, both the European Commission and a number of Member States, the World Bank and the US have cooperation programmes ongoing with China in the areas of environment and energy. First concerned are technical pilot projects, for instance, for more efficient energy use, water treatment and river basin management; second, in particular with the EU extensive cooperation is ongoing on regulatory aspects. Emissions standards for private cars in Chinese cities are, for instance, based on EU standards. These efforts, laudable and useful as they are, are obviously limited in scope. Eventually it will be China itself which will have to do the job.

When the issue of the environment is raised in diplomatic contacts the Chinese like to distinguish between *survival emissions* (with which they mean the absolutely inevitable minimum), *development emissions* (required for economic growth as in the case of China) *and luxury emissions* (emissions caused by rich countries in their pursuit of luxury consumption). The energy and pollution issue is large and looming, but the challenge is about much more than energy alone. For a number of years China's exports of cheap manufactured products had a lowering effect on inflation world wide, today the additional demand for resources from emerging economies contributes to upward pressure on prices ("*if China sells it prices go down, if China buys it prices go up*" as a participant at a "The Rise of China" conference remarked).

The appetite for resources of China's — and other emerging countries' — growth machine has contributed to higher prices for practically all commodities. Let me add: this so because the appetite of the rich countries, still by far the most important consumers of these resources, has remained large as ever. In late April 2008, The Economist's food commodity-price index, in US dollars, had increased by 69 percent compared with one year earlier, the overall commodity index by 31 percent. The on-going fall of the dollar tends to overstate these price rises, but also in euro terms the figures were high enough: 46 percent (for food) and 13 percent (all commodities) respectively.

If recession were to spread prices may come down but long-term price trends seem to be upward rather than downward, whether it concerns energy sources, iron ore, steel, bauxite, wood, rice or wheat.

"It's China" and "The China factor" sound good over the air-waves and the expressions are popular with commentators.[77] But it would be unfair and unrealistic to "blame" China and the other new-comers for today's high and rising prices of resources. It is obvious that China's growth and China's joining the club of importers of energy and other resources has contributed to the increase of prices of oil and other energy sources and raw materials (until 1994, China was a net exporter of oil). Concluding that this marginal effect — the extra, additional demand from China — is the *cause* of the problem is like blaming the passengers that stepped last on the train for the train being jam-packed (or the last-born child in the family that there is not enough food on the table).

US President Bush drew angry reactions in India when, refer-ring to India's growing middle class, he made the unfortunate remark that "when you start getting wealth, you start demanding better nutrition and better food, and so demand is high, and that causes the price to go up". People in India had a point when they reacted to this one-dimensional view saying "Why do the Americans think they deserve to eat more than Indians?" and "Instead of blaming India and other developing nations for the rise in food prices, Americans should rethink their energy policy and go on a diet"[78]

To put things further in perspective, in the area of food China is for the moment still a small exporter of rice and self-sufficient in wheat. As an importer of food China is at present less important than Egypt. This said it can only be a matter of time until eventually China will have to import foodstuffs on a much larger scale.[79] To conclude, the

---

[77] Until today articles and books are being published in which "the China price" refers to China's *low* prices because of its low labour costs.

[78] *International Herald Tribune*, 14 May, 2008.

[79] Most recently China is seeking to develop agricultural projects abroad (e.g., in Australia and Tanzania).

environmental challenge resulting from the growth of China has important internal and external implications:

- Internal: the health and well-being of the population and by implication the legitimacy of the leadership of the party and, consequently, the political stability of the country if and when pollution and environmental degradation reaches unacceptable levels.
- External: first, the direct "export" of polluted air and water;[80] second, the impact China's growing use of resources inevitably has on demand and prices of resources world-wide, but, once again, this is not something China should be "blamed" for.

III.2. Is This Sustainable: New Scarcities and the Return of Inflation

In the previous section I elaborated on the environmental challenges China is facing. I also hinted at the wider implications for the rest of the world of these challenges and of China's need for resources, given that China's demand comes *in addition* to the huge appetite for these resources that will continue to exist in today's rich nations. Looking more closely at this we will, again, have to consider too the consequences of the emergence of India and other Asian nations. The year 2008 seems to mark a turning point. The signs are that we see the beginning of a new period of much wider concern about the scarcity of resources. This scarcity was reflected by sudden price rises which are not expected to ease soon, if at all. The first months of the year brought constant news about rising prices for food, oil, coal and other resources. Some of these prices have doubled in the span of less than one year. As things stand today, it is difficult not to believe that the time of low inflation brought along by Asia's low labour costs and increased international trade is over.

On 8 May, 2008, after a period of some months, when at the heels of the financial crisis in the US the main concern was economic

---

[80] China is said to be the cause of at least 25 percent of air pollution on the US West Coast.

growth, IMF Deputy Director J. Lipsky warned that "The prospect for continued relatively strong growth in emerging and developing economies suggests that demand growth for energy and commodities will remain solid, even as global growth is slowing". He called for "a strong policy response by governments around the world to address commodity supply bottlenecks and longer-term supply issues while tackling inflationary risks".[81]

So, after years of receiving relatively little attention, inflation was back on top of the international agenda. It is not so surprising with food riots in at least a dozen of places, food hoarding taking place and rice and wheat exporting countries putting curbs on their exports (which has led to further price rises). Officials of international institutions have called on the rich countries to help the poor for whom these price rises mean ever greater or renewed poverty. There is the suggestion that today's price rises may "wipe out" everything that was achieved in the fight against poverty in the last decade. To be fair, before the IMF issued its warning the usually cautious — "conservative" — European Central Bank had, ahead of the curve, already indicated that inflation rather than economic growth was its main concern, not always with the consent of Europe's political leaders.

It would seem that the ECB was better aware of the risks ahead than its more untroubled and perhaps less knowledgeable political critics. And better aware too than the, it seems, ever optimistic managers at the helm of the US Federal Reserve Bank, who continued an inflationary policy of below zero real interest rates even in a climate of renewed and rising inflation.

With hindsight most surprising is perhaps how much this sudden general price rise came as a surprise. Among the constraints on the supply side one can think of the following: 1) drought and other bad weather conditions in some places; 2) higher energy prices, in particular, oil, which led to a steep increase in the price of fertiliser; and energy is a more general input for food production as a provider of

---

[81] http://www.imf.org/external/pubs/ft/survey/50/2008/POL0S0808A.htm

power and transport; 3) lower investment in agriculture, including agricultural research.

To the extent that higher energy prices are the explanation, it is not easy to see how these prices might come down any time soon and, therefore, how their effect on food prices can be mitigated. It would mean that input prices for farmers have increased. If marginal farmers lack the funding, partly because government interventions in the market have limited price increases, as it is suggested, supply may not sufficiently react to the constraints in the market.

Among the factors leading to higher demand most often mentioned are the following: 1) "new" demand from China and other emerging countries (which comes, we shouldn't forget, in addition to continuously high demand by rich countries, which were already important consumers); 2) "new" demand, because of diet changes as incomes rise (meat requires relatively high grain inputs; the same "in addition to" asunder (1) applies); 3) the sudden demand for bio-fuels; 4) speculation.

There may be a relationship between the first two of these demand factors ("China" and diets) and this *sudden* price shock. However, the economies of China and others have been growing for more than a decade and the Chinese and those living in other emerging economies have not all of a sudden become richer and all of a sudden started eating meat. One may of course consider that over time the extra demand explained by these factors may have led to greater strains on food markets more in general, which has made these markets more sensitive for shocks. However, pursuing the China factor, China's food imports have not increased in the last few years, nor have its food exports decreased. As I pointed out already, on the international food market China is a less important player than Egypt.

Also the possible role of drought and bad weather is not so straightforward. Rice harvests have fallen somewhat, but the world "produced a record 656 million tonnes of wheat in the year starting in July, up 8.2 percent on the previous year — although this may not be enough to restore a comfortable supply buffer to the world market. Global wheat stocks have shrunk to their lowest level since

1978".[82] On the other hand, the fairly *sudden* increase of demand, because of the recent policy choice for bio-fuels in many countries, in particular in the EU and the US, seems a not unlikely candidate for explaining higher food prices.

It has only been since recently that countries have started championing the case for bio-fuels. Initially there was great optimism about bio-fuels, although the impact of bio-fuels during their whole lifecycle had not been researched very thoroughly yet. There were not many who warned that using food as vehicle fuel might have an effect on food prices, but the tide seems to be turning now, perhaps also too suddenly. In April, 2008, the United Nations' special rapporteur for the right to food described bio-fuels as "a crime against humanity". Policy makers in the EU and the US have restated their firm commitment to bio-fuels, although bio-fuels are increasingly seen if not as the main culprit then at least as very likely accomplice:

> "For an industry that until recently was almost universally lauded as beneficial for mankind — and which is still showered with largesse from the public purse — the past year has produced a volte-face in public perception. Thanks to heavy subsidies, one-third of this year's US corn crop is forecast to be turned into vehicle fuel. At the same time, the world's poor are reeling from spiralling food prices, not the last of which being a 78 percent rise in corn prices. The situation appears to be unsustainable and the first signs of an official backlash are emerging."[83]

The recent concerns have led to greater attention for the secondary and overall effects of bio-fuels, such as the environmental consequences of land clearing and transport costs involved. Greater attention is given now to what is called the second generation bio-fuels, which are not produced from foodstuffs, but, for instance, waste. In time the supply of bio-fuels should be entirely de-coupled from the food chain.

---

[82] Chris Flood, Grains to reach record levels, *Financial Times*, 11 May, 2008.
[83] Steve Johnson, Enthusiasm for bio-fuels is questioned, *Financial Times*, 5 May, 2008.

As for agriculture investment and agriculture research the years of cheap food have indeed led to complacency and a reduction of research budgets. Lastly, speculation is mentioned as a factor driving up prices. It is suggested that after the so-called dot.com bubble and housing crisis in the US, food would now be the next bubble, in part created by the US Federal Reserve Board's inflationary policy. In a sense and in spite of today's serious disruptions this might be seen as relatively good news. If it is indeed speculation which drives these prices, it would mean that they would one day come down again and that today's high prices are not the reflection of an underlying renewed scarcity. But this may be too optimistic an assessment. Against the speculation argument pleads the fact that stocks of foodstuffs kept in warehouses are decreasing. However, given the complexity of today's financial markets, with derivative products and derivatives of derivatives, which are sometimes difficult to understand even for insiders, speculation can not be excluded as a factor.

So the jury may still be out on the precise explanation of these higher food prices, but it seems important to increase supply, improve agriculture research and thoroughly reconsider the issue of bio-fuels. We saw that it is generally thought that these higher prices indicate a trend. This trend would then reflect new scarcities, new "limits to growth". Higher prices should, however, in the longer term also create the right incentives to trigger corrective mechanisms. Soaring oil prices, for instance, are the right incentive for energy saving measures and the search for alternative energy sources. To the extent that the use of bio-fuels contribute to today's rising food prices also in this area price adjustments and policy measures should be able to correct the situation. These corrections will take time, however, and will not solve today's direct problem of high food prices for the poor. At today's juxtaposition and given the dilemmas, interactions and new questions it is difficult not to think of the pessimistic views of Thomas Malthus two centuries ago:

> The power of population is so superior to the power of the earth
> to produce subsistence for man that premature death must in some

shape or other visit the human race. The vices of mankind are active and able ministers of depopulation. They are the precursors in the great army of destruction, and often finish the dreadful work themselves. But should they fail in this war of extermination, sickly seasons, epidemics, pestilence, and plague advance in terrific array, and sweep off their thousands and tens of thousands. Should success be still incomplete, gigantic inevitable famine stalks in the rear and with one mighty blow levels the population with the food of the world.[84]

After Malthus a decline of birth rates, technological progress with higher yields in agriculture led to a continuous improvement of economic prosperity and to the belief that his prediction had been too pessimistic. In 1972, The Club of Rome published its alarmist report about pollution and the exhaustion of the world's resources — it was Malthus revisited and updated.[85] The oil price shock that followed one year later seemed to prove the Club of Rome right. But higher prices and technological progress led to the exploration of new reserves, greater energy efficiency had a mitigating effect on energy demand and improved agricultural methods led to higher yields. Once again, the concerns assuaged in subsequent years. In spite of the Club of Rome's predictions for a long period commodity prices did not rise or were even declining. So do we know if Malthus and the Club of Rome are back today or if we are we seeing no more than a hiccup in a trend of ever improving living standards and affordable costs?

III.3. Is This Sustainable: Nine Billion People and Three Billion Cars in 2050?

Today's world population is 6.6 billion who share a GDP (at PPP) of USD 66 trillion, USD 10,000 per head. On current development trends we might end up with a world population of nine billion in 2050

---

[84] Thomas Malthus, *An essay on the principles of population*, 1798 (revised five times during 1798–1826).
[85] D.L. Meadows, J. Randers, W.W. Behrens, *Limits to Growth*, 1972.

and an annual world GDP of five to six times today's, say USD 350 trillion. We arrive at this staggering amount when we assume that economic progress and development continue: we get this USD 350 trillion if we assume a growth rate for world GDP of 4 percent per year, an arbitrary but not implausible assumption. This would mean a GDP per head of USD 40,000 (in today's dollar values at PPP), almost exactly the average of GDP per head of the EU and the US today.

We may expect that these nine billion people in 2050 will want to drive cars (barring fundamental changes in transport systems they might have at least three billion cars among them), eat meat and have central heating or air conditioners. Therefore, the much bigger question than today's bickering over Chinese bras or shoes or over jobs for under-educated American steelworkers is whether this can all be achieved in a sustainable way and if so how.

Today's concerns about climate change and the recent surge in prices of resources suggest that we may have entered an era of renewed scarcity and price rises which will both require and spur adjustments in the economic and regulatory sphere, and may lead to technological breakthroughs in energy, agriculture, food production, transportation and infrastructure. Such breakthroughs do not necessarily imply new inventions, but could concern the improvement and application (or wider application) of techniques, which are already known. Existing techniques may not have been fully exploited, because they were resisted or considered too expensive as prices in the past.

The concern about emissions and climate change, which met with resistance has led to a re-think of nuclear energy. Similarly, today's rising food prices may lead to a re-think of genetically modified food, which has, so far, been met with resistance in many quarters. Too solar energy is still too expensive an alternative and accounts for no more than a fraction of today's energy supply, but prices of oil and coal are rapidly rising whereas solar panels are becoming cheaper. China is the world's largest producer of solar cell panels, but because of their high price practically all of them are exported to richer countries.

China's environmental challenge today is reminiscent of the early stages of industrialisation in Britain, the US and other early starters.

The difference is that considerable more advanced technology is available, which, however, comes at a price. A clean or cleaner environment is to an extent, like some argue for democracy, a luxury good that can only be afforded at a later stage of economic development after the most pressing material needs have been fulfilled. This has after all been the path followed by the countries that are rich today.

But the globe's capacity for producing resources and absorbing waste may not allow for another three or four billion people to follow that same "dirty growth" path. To reiterate the example given above: even if the "new fast growers" were to participate in the Kyoto emission scheme and reduce their emissions, this would only help mitigate the annual *flow of new emissions*, at best to half of today's emissions. The stock of greenhouse gases already amassed and which is mostly held responsible for climate change, would continue expanding. The UNDP Human Development Report 2007/2008 is full of evidence and warnings: "Climate change confronts humanity with stark choices. We can avoid 21st Century reversals in human development and catastrophic risks for future generations, but only by choosing to act with a sense of urgency".[86]

The risks and dilemmas we are faced with are extensively dealt with in the UNDP's "Human Development Report 2007/2008 and in Jeffrey Sachs' (JS) "Common Wealth". Both the UNDP Report and JS are, unlike Malthus, relatively optimistic in that they don't take doom for granted. Yes, the risks are very serious and time is running out, but, the message is that if we act now the tide can be reversed. "We have arrived at a narrow window of opportunity" it says in the foreword of Sachs' book.

For many years throughout the 19th century and above all during the first decades after the Second World War for those living in the rich and ever growing economies of the West it was not very difficult to believe or at least expect and hope that Malthus was wrong and that technology could solve all problems of mankind. A warning which mitigated this optimism and which is credited with marking the

---

[86] UNDP, *Human Development Report* 2007/2008, November, 2007.

beginning of the modern environmental movement, was Rachel Carson's "Silent Spring", published in 1962. The book warned more specifically against the unlimited use of chemicals, in particular, DDT, and dimmed the unlimited belief in technology.

Subsequently, in 1972 the Club of Rome's thorough and wide-ranging "Limits to Growth" implied a renewed, more general warning against man's exploitation of the earth and the risk of environmental disaster. Detailed calculations were presented demonstrating mankind's overutilization of resources and projections of their depletion. Like Malthus, the Club of Rome saw its cause weakened, however, because the world economy continued growing and the predicted price explosions and doom did not happen. Instead, after an initial economic downturn, followed by an oil crisis and rising oil prices in 1973, which for a moment seemed to prove the Club of Rome "right", world economic growth resumed.

The rise in demand for resources as projected by the Club of Rome was mitigated through price corrections for goods which were traded in functioning markets. In addition, technology continued to improve, emissions were reduced and energy efficiency increased. Consequently, resources and raw materials appeared to be plenty and policy makers and the public at large shrugged off the doom scenario. Even in road transport and urban transport where citizens increasingly and on a daily basis were confronted with congestion and pollution, there were at best flirtations with fundamental changes. In the 1960's and 1970's there were futuristic projections around of small individual electric cars which were to transport people over super-fast rail systems. Today's traffic and person transportation systems are not fundamentally different from those 30 years ago, though. The futuristic designs have remained just designs.

Environmental concern is coined "climate change" today. The EU, in particular, has pushed for climate change to be on top of the international agenda. Developments in early 2008 have led food to bypass climate change on that agenda and become the primary concern. But both, climate change and rising food prices are the reflection of today's renewed scarcity of resources, whether it be fuel, food, fertile soil or clean water and fresh air.

Annual carbon dioxide emissions per capita, 2004

Economy	CO2/head, tonnes
US	20.6
China	3.8
India	1.2
Japan	9.9
EU	8.1
Germany	9.8
UK	9.8
Italy	9.7
France	6.0
Brazil	1.8
OECD	11.5
Developing Countries	2.4
World	4.4

Source: UNDP Human Development Report, 2007/2008.

III.4. The Environment: What can be Done?

Today's attitude and debate surrounding climate change or global warming, as the overall environmental challenge is summarised and coined now, is different from 1795, 1962 and 1972 in at least two respects. At present, and, with the exception of a few pockets of ignorance or denial, there is a much more global acceptance that we are faced with a serious, long-term problem. This is an improvement, but only in part. It also implies that abundant lip service is paid to "very serious concerns" about our global or "carbon footprint". Participants to conferences on global warming, just flown in on transcontinental flights, take care to indicate to hotel staff that their towels can be re-used.

At the same time, optimism seems to prevail, however. The general perception is that the problem can be solved with step-by-step measures and above all with new technologies. Given the broad acceptance that there is a problem it seems at first sight surprising how relatively little most people are willing to do, let alone sacrifice to improve the situation. But it is perhaps precisely this prevailing optimism and the hope that technology will solve our problems, which makes people think that nothing special or major needs to be done at a personal level today. Let us hope that the optimists will prove to be right once again.

In the opening sentences of his "Common Wealth" Jeffrey Sachs, whom I would qualify as a moderate, realistic optimist says:

> The twenty-first century will overturn many of our basic assumptions about economic life. The twentieth century saw the end of European dominance of global politics and economics. The twenty-first century will see the end of American dominance. New powers, including China, India and Brazil, will continue to grow and will make their voices increasingly heard on the world stage. Yet the changes will be even deeper than a rebalancing of economics and politics among different parts of the world. The challenges of sustainable development — protecting the environment, stabilizing the world's population, narrowing the gaps between rich and poor, and ending extreme poverty — will take centre stage. Global cooperation will have to come to the fore. The very idea of nation-states that scramble for markets, power, and resources will become passé. The idea that the United States can bully or attack its way to security has proved to be misguided and self-defeating. The world has become much too crowded and dangerous for more 'great games' in the Middle East or anywhere else.[87]

Populations are growing. To mention just one example: India's population is increasing by 18 million per year. The number happens to be equal to the whole population of Australia. More people and higher incomes increase the pressure on resources. Over the last century the temperature on the globe has increased by 0.7 °C. Even if greenhouse gases in the atmosphere were to stabilise today, temperatures would continue to rise because of delayed effects. But instead of stabilisation, let alone decrease, the best thing we are

---

[87] J. Sachs, *Common Wealth, Economics for a Crowded Planet*, 2008.

talking about today is *reducing new flows, which add to the stock* of greenhouse gases that are already there. The talk and reality are not about less, but only about less extra.

My starting point has been China and I therefore cannot resist giving another quote from "Common Wealth", also because it underscores a number of points I have made above:

> China's economic rise, while improving the well-being of hundreds of millions of people, exemplifies the kind of global stresses that will be pervasive in the coming decades. It is unfair in a way to single out China for following in the well-trodden path of the rich countries, being no more or less guilty of environmental harm, but the scale and rapidity of China's economic ascent make the country's global environmental impact especially vivid. China is already causing massive global change, and much more is to come. China is currently adding the equivalent of two 500 mega-watt coal-fired plants per week, equivalent in a year the total capacity of the UK power grid. The effects on global climate change are huge.

Sachs continues with four more examples of China's rising demand for resources, each of which include the word "huge" or "massive": 1) import of soybean from Brazil, largely for animal feed, in response to a boom in meat consumption; 2) import of tropical hardwood to support the boom in residential construction; 3) import of oil with possible knock-on effects, such as land clearing for corn-based ethanol to substitute for high-cost petroleum; 4) import of exotic animal products.

The above puts it clearly enough, but what should we do, what can be done? Once more I turn to Jeffrey Sachs, who concludes "to manage the carbon budget, we don't need to change everything about our society, but we need to face head-on six important activities" (again from his Common Wealth), which are the following: "We must:

- slow or stop deforestation
- reduce emissions from electricity production
- reduce emissions from automobiles

- clean up industrial processes in a few major sectors (especially steel, cement, refineries, and petrochemicals)
- economise on electricity use through more efficient motors, appliances, lighting, insulation and other electrical demands
- convert point-source emissions in buildings (such as furnaces) into electricity-based systems powered by low-emission electricity"

This agenda is fairly precise and with today's concerns and the attitude towards climate change I don't exclude that much can be achieved in the next decades. The question that remains is whether it will be sufficient. The few recent improvements in passenger transport that possibly deserve the label "fundamental" are the emergence of high-speed trains so far mainly in Europe, spearheaded by France, and Japan, and low-budget mass air transport. But the latter development adds to emissions rather than that it reduces anything. Given Asia's urbanisation and rapidly developing cities it seems important that more innovative transportation systems are developed than the rich West has been able to come up with.

The signs, however, are rather that Asia's cities and mega-cities will follow the Western path of mass transportation with individual cars and the related mass congestion. Singapore is probably one of the very few exceptions with its combination of excellent public transport, including accessible taxis at an affordable price, considerable taxes on car ownership and the pricing of private vehicle *use* during peak hours.[88] This "Singapore solution" has produced an attractive, manageable passenger transport system. But let me be clear that in spite of this advanced system Singapore is in the same carbon footprint league as other countries with the same income level.

The rich countries demonstrate that the one-car-for-everybody model is tempting and most emerging economies are adopting this model practically automatically and without much fundamental discussion, which is making the challenge of emissions ever bigger.

---

[88] A model like Singapore's Electronic Road Pricing (ERP) system has been discussed in the Netherlands for more than 30 years; but as yet the country has been unable to begin implementation.

According to the UNDP Human Development Report 2007/2008, "the automobile sector accounts for 30 percent of greenhouse gas emissions in developing countries — and the share is rising". However, whereas the EU and the US have committed themselves to renewable fuels imports of Brazilian ethanol, which is more efficient than ethanol produced in the EU and the US, "is restricted by high import tariffs. Removing these tariffs would generate gains not just in Brazil, but for climate change mitigation" (UNDP HD Report). Apparently it has taken the farm lobbies in the EU and the US very little time to hijack the bio-fuel agenda.

The above notwithstanding, China and other emerging countries are aware that change is needed and China in particular "shops around" looking for "models" and comparing them. EU experts are intensively cooperating with China on issues such as energy security and energy efficiency. The EU has a climate change partnership with China and cooperates with China on Near Zero-Emissions Coal technology. Both the EU and China are convinced that any deal on the issue should be made within the context of the United Nations.

The fight against climate change has become the EU's top "foreign policy product". The UNDP Development Report says "The European Union's commitment to a 20–30 percent cut in emissions by 2020 would help to align carbon market with mitigation goals". Another silver lining is that with modest adjustments households in rich countries should be able to reduce their electricity use by at least one quarter. The doubt that continues haunting me, however, is, once again, that all the above is about *slowing* the process — which is good and helpful — but will it be good and helpful enough in the long-term? Only time can tell. Part of the outcome will depend on the attitude the biggest polluter of all, the US, is willing to take and the contribution it is willing to make.

III.5. The US: A "Responsible Stakeholder" Again?

On 8 December, 2005, in a speech at the conclusion of the Second US-China Senior Dialogue, Robert Zoellick, then the US Deputy Secretary of State said: "We are encouraging China to become a responsible stakeholder that will work with the United States and others to sustain, adapt and advance the peaceful international system that has enabled its success."

For an emerging country, which is just discovering the international diplomatic game and is facing very serious development challenges (large-scale poverty, pollution, huge income disparities) China, although far from being perfect, has done relatively well within that system. China has been instrumental in finding a solution for the problem of North Korea, it has concluded a "climate change pact" with the EU (the US hasn't yet) and has been supportive in the EU's efforts to find common ground with Iran. Or to take another example, when it comes to China's relationship with Taiwan, which it considers part of its territory, China has shown restraint.[89] After the change of government in Taiwan in May 2008, and the resumption of talks between the two sides soon afterwards, the prospect that the China/Taiwan question can be managed in a peaceful way is better than it has been in a decade.

Also encouraging are China's regional co-operation initiatives, such as the Shanghai Co-operation Organisation, and the fact that China's relations with its three big neighbours, India, Japan and Russia, have improved considerably. How much better are these relations than only a few years ago! True, a number of Western conservatives look at these overtures between the four Asian giants with suspicion and with regard to the warming of relations between China and Russia there is speak of an "axis of authoritarian regimes". However, just like a stable and prosperous China can only be in the interest of the West, so is a stable and prosperous Asia. It is difficult to see what benefit the West could have from instability (or worse) on the Euro-Asia continent. Why the suspicion and the concern? It seems inconsistent if not downright hypocritical to worry when relations between China and Japan or India are not good, and to worry too when these relations improve.

---

[89] The constructive, well-balanced role of the US in the cross-Strait question, through persistent, quiet diplomacy, in particular in its dealings with Taiwan, has remained largely unnoticed.

China is being criticised for its faltering in Sudan. Its role in Africa more in general certainly gives a mixed picture at best and in some cases the term "new colonialism" seems apt. But the West, I should rather say "Europe" in this case, has even after several centuries experience not yet figured out how it can play a really thoroughly useful role in Africa. Some modesty on the side of the West (Europe) would seem appropriate. Fareed Zakaria's quote of "a young Chinese official in 2006"[90] illustrates why China so often complains the West applies double standards: "When you tell us that we support a dictatorship in Sudan to have access to its oil (...) what I want to say is 'And how is that different from your support for a medieval monarchy in Saudi Arabia'." Let me add to this the voice of Rwandan President Kagame on the matter: "in the end it is up to African countries and their leaders, not the West or China, to define the terms under which they want to cooperate with China and/or the West".[91]

Back in 2005, Mr. Zoellick called on China, and he was right to do so, but the next question is: can the US still be considered a "responsible stakeholder"? Is the US, the economically most advanced and richest state on earth setting the right example? The US may call on China to "sustain, adapt and advance the peaceful international system", but the US itself walks away from that system time and again. Its commander in chief has openly defended torture, which came as a shock for many who were used to see the US as a key defender of democracy and human rights or at least pretending it was. The administration of the richest nation on earth has demonstrated its disdain for the internationally agreed Kyoto protocol for the reduction of greenhouse gases. With this policy the US provides poorer nations with the perfect excuse to ask "so why should we?".

Yes, indeed, why would they, if the US, which is six or seven or ten times richer as, say, China, and polluting four times as much per head of its population, claims it cannot afford to apply the Kyoto requirements (and doesn't offer a serious alternative either)? The US

---

[90] F. Zakaria, *The Post–American World*, 2008.

[91] As Rwandan President Paul Kagame stressed, during a public presentation in Singapore on 22 May, 2008 (his remark led to enthusiastic applause from the audience).

claims to be the defender of international justice and democracy and is prepared to go to war over these principles, but at the same time it has refused to support the landmark agreement on the International Criminal Court of Justice. Opinion polls worldwide show a considerable drop in respect for and popularity of the US, above all, in the Islamic world, but also in Europe.

In an article in "Foreign Affairs", of early 2008, G.J. Ikenberry gives an overly optimistic view of the US as a good-doer and the positive influence of the US on world affairs.[92] China will be welcome to join the open, liberal system created by the US, he says, but, he wonders if China will want to join as a responsible player. "Will China overthrow the existing order or become part of it? And what, if anything, can the United States do to maintain its position as China rises?" Ikenberry wonders. He continues: "China faces an international order that is fundamentally different from those that past rising states confronted. China does not just face the United States; it faces a Western-centred system that is open, integrated and rule-based, with wide and deep political foundations."

Ikenberry is right reminding us how the US was at the cradle of some of today's international institutions and how America's lead role and those institutions helped Germany and Japan integrate and normalise; how, after the Cold War, the Western order managed to assuage Russia's concerns (although one may claim that the West's pushing it too far in the 1990's has led to a backlash today) and accomplished the integration of a new wave of countries from the formerly communist world. It certainly is worth remembering this. However, neither Ikenberry nor most other American authors seem to realise that America's more recent attitude and behaviour on the international stage have led to an erosion of the trust in the US the rest of the world used to have. The world has started wondering about America's commitment to the good cause, to international institutions, to international law and international co-operation.

---

[92] G.J. Ikenberry, *The Rise of China and the Future of the West*, in *Foreign Affairs*, January/February, 2008.

Jeffrey Sachs reminds us usefully that these recent "negatives" are *not* an entirely new development from a benign US to a bad US (my paraphrase). He uses the expression "the two faces of US foreign policy". One is the face as pictured by Ikenberry: an engaging US, Roosevelt, the United Nations, the Bretton Woods Institutions and the US Peace Corps. On the other face we see covert CIA actions, the overthrow of regimes in South America, Iran, Vietnam:

> There have long been two faces of US foreign policy. Since the United States became a great global power after World War II, US foreign policy has veered between the visionary cooperation of Kennedy's Partial Test Ban Treaty and the reckless unilateralism of the CIA-sponsored invasion of Cuba that preceded it. Great acts of US cooperative leadership include the establishment of the UN, the IMF and World Bank, the promotion of an open global trading system, the Marshall Plan to fund European reconstruction, the eradication of smallpox, the promotion of nuclear arms control, and the elimination of ozone-depleting chemicals. Notorious acts of US unilateralism include the CIA-led overthrows of several governments (Iran, Guyana, Guatemala, South Vietnam, Chile), the assassination of countless foreign officials, and several disastrous unilateral acts of war (in Central America, Vietnam, Cambodia, Laos and Iraq). (...) The Bush administration's unilateralism therefore has deep roots in once facet of American foreign policy, but its crudeness and violence are unprecedented. ("Common Wealth", 2008)

In the first decades after the World War II the US was a main force pushing co-operation in Europe and supporting and encouraging the creation of the European Union. At present, one gets the impression that America seeks to undermine existing international arrangements rather than to reinforce them. American magazine Newsweek's comment to a speech by US Senator John McCain, the Republican candidate for the US presidency, in which the latter called for a League of Democratic Nations, was the following:

> "(according to McCain) The United States should adopt a policy of active exclusion and hostility toward two major global powers. It would reverse a decades-old bipartisan American policy of integrating these two countries into the global order; a policy that began with Richard Nixon (with Beijing) and continued under Ronald Reagan (with Moscow). It is a policy that would alienate many countries in Europe and Asia who would see it as an attempt by Washington to begin a new Cold War."[93]

What is the need for this new international organisation? Would democracies such as, for instance, India, Brazil or Indonesia, be willing to join this League? One of the most important questions for the future of the globe is if the US can accept international rules again, be a "responsible stakeholder" in a multilateral world and lead by example in the UN and other international organisations also if this may mean that the US does not automatically get its way. What could such a new organisation contribute to that question?

What would there be to talk about by the like-minded democracies in this League of democracies? Should they have meetings to congratulate each other and celebrate? Who should be invited? If we take Freedom House's Democracy Audit as our guide,[94] should we stop at the "first division", at Poland, democracy number 29 on the list? This would mean that Japan and Greece would be excluded. Or should the second division be included too? Or also the third division, which would mean that Sierra Leone, number 73 on Freedom House's list, would be the last one to be invited? The proposal for this League is put forward in Robert Kagan's "The Return of History,[95] which starts

---

[93] F. Zakaria, "*McCain versus McCain*", in Newsweek, 5 May, 2008.
[94] www.worldaudit.og/democracy.htm
[95] R. Kagan, *The Return of History and the End of Dreams*, 2008.

of with the infantile notion — and takes it as its premise — that in the early 1990's "we" lived "the end of history". From 1994 to 1998 I lived and worked in Poland to assist that country in the transformation process it had so firmly embarked on. It was certainly an historic period for Poland and some in Poland felt like being part of history, but we never felt we were seeing "the end of history". History went on, as history always does, as became clear during the delicate process of Poland's joining NATO and concern for the Russian reaction at the time.

But let me get back to the subject of the environment and international cooperation. Talking environment and seriously addressing the challenge of global warming Nigel Purvis says:[96]

> But very few climate experts believe much progress can be made in narrowing the transatlantic divide on the central political question — how quickly should the major powers mitigate their emissions over the next decade? Whereas Europe proposes to reduce its emissions by 20 percent below 1990 levels by 2020 and up to 30 percent if other countries adopt similar goals, President George W. Bush believes US emissions will need to continue to rise until 2025.

The US has rejected the EU call for legally binding emission reduction targets and simply stated that it thinks that a further rise of emissions until 2025 cannot be avoided. The candidates of the US presidential race in 2008 make more promising noises, but it remains questionable whether, given America's faith driven belief that it is "owner of the earth", any proposals for the better will pass American Congress. So the question is indeed "When will the US become a responsible stakeholder again?"

---

[96] N. Purvis, Narrowing the Transatlantic Climate Divide, *The German Marshall Fund of the United States*, June 2008.

Chapter IV

China and the West, Asia and the Rest

China and Asia's "climbing the ladder" is today's big story. We have seen that over the last two centuries country after country have climbed the economic development ladder. Perhaps I have not reminded the reader sufficiently that onward improvement are not guaranteed. In the early decades of the 20th century Argentina and other South American countries were on par with Western Europe, but subsequently saw serious setbacks. Emerging countries are initially seen as a threat, but, subsequently, they join the others "up there". History often repeats itself, and, as always, politicians and lobbies in countries higher up the ladder will try to block emerging economies in their development path. Great Britain's repeal of the Corn Laws adopted by the British Parliament in 1846 is still a landmark:

> The Corn Laws, in force between 1689 and 1846, were designed to protect English landholders by encouraging the export and limiting the import of corn when prices fell below a fixed point. They were eventually abolished in the face of militant agitation by the Anti-Corn-Law-League, formed in Manchester in 1839, which maintained that the laws, which amounted to a subsidy, increased industrial costs. After a lengthy campaign, opponents of the law finally got their way in 1846 — a significant triumph which was indicative of the new political power of the English middle class.[97]

---

[97] http://en.wikipedia.org/wiki/Corn_Laws.

There will always be special interests of, for instance, agriculture producers in the US and the EU and steel producers and steelworkers and shoemakers — and, not to forget, state-owned companies in China — who will try to convince their governments that citizens should be prevented from buying abroad or have to pay an extra tax if they do. These less productive producers may be protected, but protective measures work only temporarily. Those who lose are consumers (including those who process the products concerned) in the country that imposes protective measures as they see their choices limited and their tax burden and prices going up.

More recently, American economists with a record of impeccable free-trade and economic integration credentials have come forward with second-thoughts about free-trade and globalisation. Not the least among them Noble Prize winner Paul Samuelson, former free-trade guru Paul Krugman and Larry Summers. How can it be that so much combined wisdom all of a sudden fails to see what it first thought it saw and is now professing another paradigm? "Is a liberal international economic order losing international support?" Devesh Kapur, Pratap Mehta and Arvind Subramanian wonder in the Financial Times, in reaction to an article earlier on by Mr. Summers in that same newspaper.[98] "The best line of defence for protecting workers has to be overwhelmingly domestic" they say. How right they are.

For decades American professors have been telling the world that "the proliferation of prosperity across countries was a good thing" as these three authors say. But with US economic pre-eminence challenged the professors are all of a sudden not so sure anymore. Earlier on I pointed out that globalisation and the "China threat", are in the US more a left/right issue, but this fresh support of the "converted enlightened professors" may give the anti-globalisation paradigm a new boost and acceptability in the US, a worrying perspective.

---

[98] D. Kapur, P. Mehta, A. Subramanian, Is Larry Summers the canary in the mine? *Financial Times*, 14 May, 2008.

Free-trade and economic integration are in part about "gains for most", but above all about "freedom to chose". Trade measures are like censorship. Why would the government of a country punish its citizens, let them pay extra, to give a helping hand to steel or shoe makers who have failed to adjust to international competition? Why should consumers be told by their government where it is politically correct to shop? Why should ethanol from Brazil be punished with a prohibitively high import tariff in the EU and the US whereas both these major actors have committed to make greater use of bio-fuels? The answer is that growers of rapeseed and corn for bio-fuel in the EU and the US have lobbied to protect their interests, to great effect.

China and the West, Asia and the rest is the title of this section. The focus of my story is on China and, in the same breath — or in parentheses, whatever way one wants to put it — I mention "India and Asia in general". I reiterate it several times and, for instance, Fareed Zakaria mentions it in his "Post-American World": "any number, however small, becomes a large number when multiplied by 2.5 billion (the approximate population of China plus India)". And that figure becomes three billion when the ten ASEAN countries are added up (my figure is 2.4 + 0.5 = 2.9 billion, but that comes down to the same thing). Zakaria usefully reminds that today it is no longer Asia alone. The term BRICS stands for China and India together with Brazil and Russia. More "risers" or "emergers" are joining the "global concert", be it South Africa, Kenya or Argentina. Perhaps I should have referred more to other economies that are already "there", Japan which will now hopefully be able to leave its "lost decade" definitely behind and, to mention just two, Australia and Canada, which more recently have been benefiting from booming resource markets.

In comparing the US and the EU, I mentioned the better overall distribution of knowledge and of access to education of reasonable quality in the EU and the more equal distribution of income. Let me reiterate that it is not so much China and globalisation which form a threat to unskilled labour, but today's labour has to cope with technology. Steelworkers have to be able to work with computers.

This requires knowledge, which requires appropriate long-term government policies. That is the price we pay for ever higher living standards. "Most of Europe is willing to pay that price and if things go wrong there is Europe's social security safety net. There is no short-cut to long-term prosperity. Good education and long-term competiveness require long-term investment, effort, patience and time. Protectionism is a quick fix, but works only in the short-term."[99]

Good governance leads to greater prosperity. The US should be reminded of the benefits of proper education for all and, for that matter, good infrastructure and access to affordable health care. Governor Schwarzenegger of California reportedly was impressed by the high speed of trains in France when he visited in April 2008. Roads in France are of excellent quality too. America is excellent at excelling; it is excellent at the top, but lacks in ensuring that knowledge and incomes are appropriately spread along the population, its own population, at large.

Fortunately and how could it be otherwise, the US still has its more optimistic scholars than the "converted professors". Examples are Thomas Friedman and Fareed Zakaria. The latter argues that for the US:

> The potential for a new burst of American productivity depends not on our education system or R&D spending, but on our immigration policy. If these people (*note:* foreign students and immigrants who account for almost 50 percent of all science researchers in the US) are allowed and encouraged to stay, then innovation will happen here. If they leave, they'll take it with them. More broadly, this is America's great — and potentially insurmountable — strength. It remains the most open, flexible society in the world, able to absorb other people, cultures, ideas, goods and services. The country thrives on the hunger and energy of poor immigrants. Faced with the new technologies of foreign companies, or growing markets overseas, it adapts and adjusts. When you compare this dynamism with the closed and hierarchical nations that were once superpowers, you

---

[99] J.W. Blankert, Focus on tech challenge — not China threat, *Financial Times*, 20 May, 2008.

sense that the United States is different and may not fall in the trap of becoming rich, and fat, and lazy.[100]

Zakaria's hailing of immigration should be seen against the backdrop of the serious shortages of engineers and other professionals, technology exporters Germany and Japan are facing, two countries with a less enlightened immigration policy than the US. If Germany and Japan want to continue producing and exporting their top-quality products they will have to accept the immigration of high-quality foreign labour. But, most importantly, Zakaria reminds us that in essence we are competing with ourselves. For economic progress continuous productivity improvement is required, irrespective what others are doing.

The West should respond effectively to China's (and Asia's) renewed strength. One of the EU's explicit policy priorities in its dealings with China is to support China's emergence as a successful and responsible member of the international community. The way the EU seeks to achieve this is through *engagement and partnership.* The objective is that both benefit from the partnership. It is inevitable that some in the West feel insecure about China's increasing economic strength and competitive capacity. However, the lessons from history show us, that closing the doors in response to competition is not the right answer. Renewed protectionism and a defensive attitude can only backfire. Moreover, China and the rest of Asia will rise anyway, whether with the West or without.

In the first part of this text we saw how it is first and foremost countries' economic policy and institutions that bring economic growth and prosperity. In the same vein, it is economic policy and institutions — education, research and development with social security providing a safety net (and for the many aging economies we may add immigration as a factor too) — which should provide further economic progress. The West needs to find and develop its areas of comparative advantage and, where necessary help workers to retrain.

---

[100] F. Zakaria, The Rise of the Rest, in *Newsweek*, 12 May, 2008.

The West's response to China's (India's, Asia's) rise should be improving its own competitiveness, improving education and the flexibility of markets. The US should reinforce its primary and secondary education system, the EU, in particular its university education, including the support to research and development. China's rise serves the EU and its Member States by reminding them of the importance to implement and complete the Lisbon Agenda for improving competitiveness. And let Zakaria's remark about immigration remind us that also for the EU immigration is a delicate issue, which needs careful management.

The EU actively supports China's internal political and economic reform process. The European Commission's Communication on China of October 2006 says: "a strong and stable China which fully respects fundamental rights, and freedoms, protects minorities and guarantees the rule of law. The EU will reinforce co-operation to ensure sustainable development, pursue a fair and robust trade policy and work together in support of peace and stability."

Officials of the European Commission have 25 so-called sectoral dialogues ongoing with their Chinese counterparts. These dialogues cover issues from civil aviation, social security and employment to regional policy, macro-economic questions and environmental protection. In the context of these dialogues regulatory issues take a prominent place. Examples are ILO standards, accounting standards, environmental standards (e.g. car emission standards). After more than ten years of discussion and stepping forward and backwards, China has finally adopted important legislation in the areas of competition (anti-trust law) and of employment (labour law). Also in these areas there has been extensive cooperation between policy experts in the European Commission and the EU in general, including experts in EU Member States, and the Chinese drafters of these laws.

With pollution, income disparities are possibly the two biggest challenges to the Chinese regime with possibly the greatest potential for social unrest. Chinese leaders are aware of this fact and look at the various income redistribution mechanisms in force in the EU, in particular, the Community Regional Policy system. This system takes now some 40 percent of the Community budget, some 0.45 percent of total GDP of the EU. In spite of its relatively modest size this fund has helped poorer regions catch up (provided the right policies were in place). China has shown a keen interest in how this system works.

One can only conclude that the West like China, India and the rest of Asia all benefit from globalisation and share common interests. Both sides should seek to enhance the multilateral systems and make them more effective. Divergences in values remain which require dialogue, but these should not interfere with cooperation in the many areas where cooperation is required, from climate change to maintaining peace. The major real, but common challenge is to achieve a further rise of living standards in a sustainable and peaceful manner. That is the main question that needs to be addressed and worked on in the next decades.

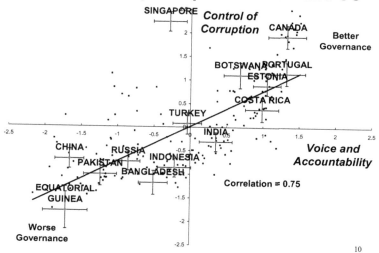

Government indicators: World Bank, D. Kaufmann, A. Kraay, M. Mastruzzi

By Tristram Hunt, THE GUARDIAN, London, Friday, Aug 04, 2006, page 9; * http://www.guardian.co.uk/commentisfree/2006/jul/28/ comment.china (for corrections and clarifications).

This is a tale of two cities. The first is Charles Dickens' Coketown: "It was a town of red brick or of brick which would have been red if the smoke and ashes had allowed it; but as matters stood it was a town of unnatural red and black like the painted face of a savage. It was a town of machinery and tall chimneys, out of which interminable serpents of smoke trailed themselves for ever and ever and never got uncoiled." The second is the Chinese city of Chongqing as described by (the *Guardian*'s) Jonathan Watts: "It is just after dawn, but the sun remains hidden behind a thick haze. The giant movement of humanity that is Chongqing is about to get into full swing, working, building, consuming, discarding, developing ... We head into the hills to see the biggest of the mega-city's rubbish mega-pits ... an awesome sight; a giant reservoir of garbage, more than 30 m deep and stretching over 350,000 m²."

After a decade of urbanization and industrialization, China's cities now resemble the nightmare metropolises of mid-19th-century Britain. Accounts of the pollution, ill-health and overcrowding in Nanjing or Chengdu recall the worst excesses of 1840s Manchester or Glasgow. Last week the Chinese authorities finally began to face up to their urban problems with the announcement of a US$178.4 billion clean-up fund. But equally telling is Beijing's recent invitation to a British 19th-century historian, Gareth Stedman Jones, to tell them just how we managed the transition to a modern urban nation.

The similarities are striking. Between 1770 and 1840 Britain underwent one of the most dramatic urban migrations in world history. Hundreds of thousands left their villages and farmsteads for the workshops of Birmingham, docks of Liverpool and mills of Manchester. Sheffield and Bradford doubled their populations in a matter of years. Today that history is repeating itself in China as families from the rural hinterland decamp for the coastal cities. Every year 8.5 million peasants make their way into the urban centers. By next year China is set to become a majority-urban nation, with more than 3.2 billion* living in cities and suburbs. With the influx of China's peasantry has come the inevitable accompaniment of low wages, exploitation and tension with the indigenous working class. In Victorian Manchester the Irish, in Glasgow the Highland crofters, and in London the Hampshire laborers, became victims of a savagely flexible labor market.

In China the underemployed urban masses are known as "bang-bang men": unskilled laborers hanging around docks and markets (as they used to in London and Liverpool) ready to do any work, however dangerous or dirty. And it certainly is dirty work. From its construction sites, factories, sweatshops and car plants, China's cities have fermented a witches' brew of environmental pollution. "A sort of black smoke covers the city. The sun seen through it is a disc without rays," wrote Alexis de Tocqueville of 1830s Manchester. The same could be said of Xinghua or Shanghai today. China is currently home to 20 of the world's 30 most smog-choked cities. And its plans for ever more motorways and airports will only make it worse.

Meanwhile, its rivers — even the once-mighty Yangtze — now resemble "the fetid, muddy waters, stained with a thousand colors by the factories they pass" of De Tocqueville's Manchester. This ever-present pollution causes chronic health problems. Just as the squalor of the Victorian city led to an explosion of cholera, typhus, typhoid and smallpox, the noxious cloud of China's cities has resulted in marked increases in lung cancer, bronchitis and other respiratory diseases. Only fears for the health of athletes competing in the 2008 Olympics has at last spurred municipalities to act in reducing levels of sulphur dioxide and dust. The initial Victorian response to the state of their cities was equally lackadaisical. Pollution and inequality was the price of progress, and the middle classes solved their problems by simply moving upwind. But in the end a combination of religion, officialdom and civil society forced the cities to change. Evangelical Christians assailed the white slavery of factory hands and demanded reforms to working hours and conditions. The growth of the state alongside the science of statistics led to a new awareness of the human cost of city living. In 1834 the Office of the Registrar-General was formed, and every year it issued mortality figures revealing the true horror of urban industrial life.

These official facts were marshalled by a new breed of interventionist civil servants, led by the public-health campaigner Edwin Chadwick, in their Whitehall campaign for state intervention. Assisting Chadwick in his struggle was a free press. The journalism of Henry Mayhew and WT Stead, alongside the novels of Dickens, Benjamin Disraeli and Elizabeth Gaskell, helped to put pressure on politicians and industrialists to clean up their conurbations. The public voice of civil society produced the great social reforms of the mid-19th century, from sewerage to child labor and trade union rights.

But in modern China there exist few if any of these reforming tendencies. The Beijing authorities have handicapped free religious expression and the social movements that come with it. The state is notoriously secretive when it comes to the release of environment statistics. Rather than leading the fight for reform, China's provincial officialdom is notorious for its incompetence and corruption. Meanwhile the Chinese Communist Party leadership continues to take an aggressively Maoist approach to civil society: non-government organizations, an open Internet and a free press are not at the top of their list of concerns.

Much to their relief, Gareth Stedman Jones argued that Britain held back the urban masses from rebellion in the early 19th century not with an immediate transfer to democracy but by cutting sales taxes, stamping on bureaucratic bribery and curbing the elite aristocracy. But such reforms were only a holding point. Ultimately the urban masses had to be enfranchised. For at the forefront of politicians' minds was another story of rapid urbanization. Across the Channel, France too was trying to cope with startling rates of immigration and industrialization. But the consequence of its political fumbling was a Paris in flames in 1830, 1848 and 1871. That is a history the Chinese are all too keen to avoid.

Chapter V

Then the World Changed: Crisis

INTERLUDE, NOVEMBER, 2008

"GLOBAL SLIDE INTO DEEP RECESSION"
"US RETAIL SALES FALL"
EURO-ZONE MANUFACTURING CONTRACTS AT RECORD SPEED"
"BAIL OUT CAR MAKERS OR FACE MASSIVE JOB CUTS"
"SPLIT WIDENS OVER EUROPEAN RECOVERY PLAN"
"MERKEL DEFENDS CAUTIOUS REPONSE TO RECESSION"
"JOB LOSSES HEIGHTEN RECESSION CONCERNS"
"OIL PRICE FALLS BELOW 50 DOLLARS"
"OVER ASIA, FOUL CLOUD SULLIES AIR AND WATER, TOXIC SMOG
ALTERS WEATHER AND DAMAGES HEALTH, UN SAY"
"EU "VERY CLOSE" TO CLIMATE PACKAGE DEAL"
"ARTIC ICE THICKNESS PLUMMETS"

"We are watching a bonfire of the old orthodoxies as well as of the vanities. This week Barack Obama promised to spend hundreds of billions of taxpayers' dollars to prop up the sinking US economy. Gordon Brown's British government announced it would soak the rich to pay for an economic rescue package. In between times the Bush administration all but nationalised Citigroup, the world's largest bank. For good measure it threw another, yet another, $800 bn into the effort to thaw US credit markets. Everywhere you look, Keynes' demand management is replacing Adam Smith's invisible hand; printing money, a mortal sin under the fracturing Washington consensus, is the new prudence. Something big is happening. What started out as a series of pragmatic ad hoc responses is moving the boundary between state and market. Politicians are now overlaying expediency with ideology. Government is no longer a term of abuse."[101]

---

[101] P. Stephens, Broken banks put the state back in the driving seat, *Financial Times*, 28 November, 2008.

V.1. World Economy in Turnmoil

In June 2008, I delivered the preceding chapters to the publisher, feeling my narrative was complete and that it was a balanced story. My publisher agreed. Let me reiterate my main points — with the second main issue here under two separate bullets, the second and third, to stress the message:

- *Long-term economic growth*: China, India and other Asian economies have only recently started emerging. It took them long to join the "race up the income ladder". Let's be happy they finally are finding the way.
- *International competition I*: the rise of China (and India and Asia in general) and the perception of threat this leads to is nothing new. Economic competition between people, industry sectors, cities, countries and regions, globalisation, has been of all times. Throughout the centuries, growth by newcomers has been accommodated. True, some suffered in the adjustment process, but most have been benefiting. Why would it be different this time?[102]
- *International competition II*: rich economies should ensure their high standards of living through high quality, broad-based education of their population, research and innovation, and appropriate economic policies to maintain balance. The productivity growth required for economic progress is above all a *domestic* matter.
- *The real challenge concerns the environment* and natural resources. The prosperity of the 20 percent richest people on earth has led to massive environmental damage. Will it be possible to accommodate the race to prosperity of the rest — several billions who also want more and better food, bigger houses, cars and proper heating or cooling systems in their homes?

In September and October 2008, while this book was being prepared for publication, the financial crisis that had been lingering for more

---

[102] A splendid book on the subject showing that globalisation has always been there, throughout the centuries is W.J. Berstein's *A Splendid Exchange*, 2008.

than a year, mostly in the US, unfolded full-scale. Tumbling banks were saved with unprecedented amounts of government funds. The emergency measures seemed to help, the banking crisis calmed, although nobody knew if it was entirely over and economic growth worldwide slowed and one western country after another went into recession. Bad financial and economic news continued, consumer and business confidence kept falling and economic forecasts were becoming bleaker by the day.

In August/September 2008 the general assumption was that by the end of 2009 economic recovery would set in. But now, as 2008 is running to its end, we can no longer exclude that it will take until well into 2010 until the major Western economies will begin to recover. Comparisons are made with the Great Depression, which set in after the Wall Street crash of 1929 and which lasted until 1933. One obvious and ominous similarity with that period at the least is today's continuous downward revisions of economic forecasts. But with these constant revisions what is the value of these forecasts? The problem is that "economists cannot predict vertical lines", collapse is not part of the economic forecasting toolbox. Considering that if not the world, the economic scene has changed in the last months my publisher proposed that I add a last chapter to this book, taking into account the "seismic changes" that are taking place. That is quite a challenge, but here we go then.

Governments may have prevented much worse with their massive bail-outs of banks and subsequent economic stimulus packages — and, in spite of criticism, demonstrating considerable and recommendable international coordination. They may have prevented a complete financial meltdown, but it is too early to tell with certainty. Each day brings further news of how the recession is widening throughout western economies. Factory orders are declining, retail sales stagnate, cars remain unsold and unemployment is rising rapidly, particularly in the US. Initially it was believed that China and other emerging economies could escape the recession. Until well into 2008, cheerful talk about "decoupling" held ground, meaning that the new emerging economies would have become more or less immune from the economies of the US and the west in general. In the meantime, we have seen they haven't. With hindsight we may also say how naïve was that thought in particular in the case of China, given China's export dependence. But things might have been worse today without the mitigating effect of the emerging economies, exactly because, as it appears now, there isn't that much decoupling to speak of. Chinese leaders maintain that "keeping the Chinese economy prospering is the best thing China can do for the world".[103]

Earlier in this book, referring to the possible effect of economic malaise in America for China and India, I said that it would be "no drama" if these countries were to end up with economic growth of 9 percent and 8 percent respectively in 2008. But also for China, India and the rest of Asia economic prospects are getting bleaker by the day and economic growth is likely to end up considerably lower than this 9 percent and 8 percent. How about 2009? Suppose that China's growth is no more than 7.5 percent next year[104] or even lower (5 percent is mentioned as a possibility). That would still be a very impressive figure by any standard, but for an economy addicted to 10 percent growth each year it would mean that millions of the extra jobs needed each year, would not be created. Factories in China are reporting major lay-offs. Job losses mean that migrant labour returns to the Chinese country side adding to the potential for instability. After originating in the west, this crisis could therefore lead to social unrest China's rural areas — as it may very well lead to social unrest in the west — so far for "decoupling".

> "If growth falls below 8 percent then that will create enormous problems in terms of unemployment" said Zhang Xiaojing, director of the Macroeconomic Office of the Institute of Economics, at the Chinese Academy of Social Sciences. "There will be lots of laid-off migrant workers returning to the villages, not to mention the many college graduates, and this will affect social stability." [...].
> He linked the continuing riots in Greece to the global economic

---

[103] China's stimulus package of $586 billion was referred to as "China's biggest contribution" to the world" (Xinhua News).
[104] *The Economist's* poll of the Economist Intelligence Unit estimate/forecast, 2 December, 2008.

crisis and said Beijing was wary of a similar situation erupting in China."[105]

"As in 1929, the world is experiencing a global contraction. It is crucially important that policymakers understand how the global balance of payments must adjust" says Michael Pattis.[106] For him overcapacity is the underlying explanation of today's crisis. In 1929 it was America's overcapacity which was at the basis of the crisis. In 1929 America "could engineer massive fiscal expansion to replace global demand, or it could close down factories and lay off workers." Instead, the US sought to stimulate demand for American products by sharply raising the cost of foreign imports through the notorious Smoot-Hawley Act. Other countries retaliated by raising their import tariffs, which made the adjustment process much longer and more painful than it had needed to be. The fundamental imbalance this time, Pattis argues, may have been America's over-consumption, but its mirror image is China's overproduction. With America's consumption bubble deflating, China should reduce capacity:

> China must reduce over-production — either by boosting domestic consumption or by closing factories. If China tries its own version of Smoot-Hawley and subsidizes the export sector by lowering costs, depreciating the currency or providing cheaper financing, it will effectively make the same mistake the United States did in 1930, try to force the adjustment abroad. This will only invite retaliation abroad.

"China must reduce over-production — either by boosting domestic consumption or by closing factories." To achieve this, Chinese leaders could finally allow the exchange rate to rise. It would mean that China would stop selling at a discount, allow Chinese workers who have a job greater prosperity and the surplus on the current account to come

---

[105] J. Anderlini, Beijing prioritises employment for graduates to head off unrest, *Financial Times*, 22 December, 2008.

[106] M. Pattis, What China can learn from 1929, *Newsweek*, 22 December, 2008.

down. But it is highly unlikely that Chinese leaders would dare to follow this path, which would lead to even larger part of Chinese factory jobs to disappear. It would further increase the risk of social unrest and instability. Another way out for China would be to boost domestic expenditure, for instance, by investing in the inadequate health care system. An overhaul of the health care system, long overdue, would seem a worthy cause for the "socialist market economy". Many could benefit, above all, the poor in China, but middle class Chinese too. Investing in the health care system would allow the Chinese people to reduce their savings. Today, serious illness can mean financial disaster for a Chinese family, which is one of the factors explaining China's excessively high savings rate. Indeed, in December 2008, in an effort to boost spending, the Chinese government announced an economic stimulus package of 586 billion US dollar. Health was not an important element of this package — which doesn't mean that the economic impact should be less. But is it enough?

In previous chapters I hint to recession fears and risks. When I wrote those chapters in the first half of 2008, only a handful of off-mainstream pundits expected economic disruption and fear on a scale as we see today. There were anxieties expressed over the high-risk games being played in the financial sector and the risks this implied for that sector as a whole. But the scale of irresponsible behaviour and, consequently, the scale of the unravelling are much larger than initially understood. Today's uncertainty and the speed by which we have arrived in this situation, so unexpectedly and unprepared, invite cynical comments like the following:

> Of course, economists' and analysts' guesses are rarely worthwhile. How many foresaw the market collapse coming? Very, very few. How many saw the price of oil below $50? Who guessed that Japanese stocks would fall 50 percent? Or that Warren Buffett would lose $25 billion? Practically no one. Analysts lack imagination. Instead, they merely read the day's news...and extrapolate. They imagine that tomorrow will be like today. Often, it is. But sometimes, it is not.[107]

---

[107] The Daily Reckoning website, http://www.dailyreckoning.com

Today's predictions and the continuous changes they undergo demonstrate the limits of economic knowledge and understanding. In August 2008, the World Bank's growth forecast for the Chinese economy in 2009 was 9.5 percent. In November that forecast was reduced to 7.5 percent. And in the meantime, one month later only, there is talk of a meagre 5 percent growth in China in 2009. A difference this size within three months time is illustrative for the limits of economic calculations, in particular, in today's uncertain situation. Is the economic profession a profession, like, say, medicine, where there are diseases and certain well-defined remedies? Perhaps not, but before rejecting all economics right away let us remember that there are also ills which it may take the medical professional a while to diagnose and there are ills too, against which the medical profession is still looking for a cure.

If economic circumstances were to worsen further, forecasts will be adjusted once again. Forecasts are "extrapolations" indeed, made on the assumption that circumstances will not change too drastically. It is like someone beginning a journey from Paris to Madrid, who when indicating expected arrival time in Madrid, implicitly assumes there will be no snowstorms, earthquakes, avalanches or floods on the way. Economic forecasters and their theories and models assume smooth lines. They see disruptions from the regular path as temporary fluctuations and aberrations after which "the system" will return to "normal".

The Wall Street crash of 1929 and the economic depression that followed — also that depression did not appear in forecasts, nor did its length — led to fundamentally new thoughts about the functioning of a market economy and a more proactive, interventionist government policy. Government employment projects were kicked off well before John Maynard Keynes published his "General theory of employment, interest rates and money", but his theory provided the economic rationale for such projects. According to the "classical" theory prevailing before Keynes, the "real economy" where people produced food and steel and cars was what mattered for the creation of wealth and employment. Somewhere above that real economy was a world of money and finance which could to some degree be helpful to make the "real economy" function, but would not be able to disrupt it. Keynes argued however that money did matter (could have an effect on wealth creation and employment), that markets could fail and that there was a clear role for government when this happened.

After five decades of, one may argue, perhaps sometimes too much emphasis on and belief in the useful role of government intervention, the 1980's brought, in particular, in the US and the UK, a renewed interest in and political push for the classical theory: more market functioning and less government intervention were promoted. The great names of this conservative "revolution" were those of the politicians Ronald Reagan and Margaret Thatcher and the economist Milton Friedman. The "new old" thinking half a century after 1929 was that governments should *not* intervene or, more accurately, limit their interventions to a minimum. Monetary policy should be strictly neutral and governments should not seek to stimulate the economy with fiscal measures. Friedman argued that markets and market agents were in all cases rational enough to regulate and control themselves and each other and should therefore be left alone. According to him, government intervention was the problem rather than the cure. In 2008, thirty years later again, Mr. Keynes's ghost has come to haunt us: we are all Keynesians now — or Keynesians again.

V.2. Crisis: Paradigm Change?

Yes "we are all Keynesians now", because even more unexpected than the economic downturn were the massive direct financial interventions by governments all over the world, also because they were without precedent. The amounts were up to one trillion US dollars in the US and two trillion euros in the EU, followed by hundreds of billions in other places, from Australia to India, from Japan to Russia and, not least, China too. To be frank, I am not sure if these figures as I give them are correct as the stimulus packages continue coming. Moreover, to complicate things further, part of these packages are no more than the re-packaging of old spending plans — or that is what sceptical analysts claim.

Other considerations about the role of the government and the usefulness of government interventions aside, were governments not supposed to limit their financial deficits — i.e., were they not supposed to limit what they spend in excess of tax revenues? Were they not supposed to keep their books balanced? Contrary to what is often assumed, Keynes has never suggested that governments could run deficits and build up debts without having to bother. Also, the US government, after, for instance, building up a considerable war debt during the World War II, to pay for exceptional costs under exceptional circumstances settled that debt once the war was over. It was only in the years of "enlightened negligence" under US presidents Reagan and later Bush that government debt was allowed to cumulate limitlessly without thinking about paying back. Yes, it sounds and it is paradoxical that these two presidents considered themselves as disciples of the doctrine that the government should limit its interventionism.

It has hardly been a decade since gradually and slowly, with the exception of the US in the last eight years, prudence in government finances became the norm, again in most western countries and in fact in the majority of mature nations. One of the fiscal policy norms within the Euro zone is that the annual government deficit (the extent to which government expenditures in a year exceed revenues) should not exceed 3 percent of GDP. But rescue packages presented so far have been up to 10 percent of GDP and even more in countries which have already considerable government debts. The debt of the US government is 75 percent of US GDP; in the EU government debts amount to 40 percent to 60 percent of GDP in the countries most concerned with stimulus expenditure packages. In relative terms China's aid package of 586 billion US dollars, 16 percent of China's GDP, is one of the largest. The Chinese government has a modest debt to GDP ratio, however, much smaller than what is usual in the West. It is estimated to be less than 25 percent, which gives China more leeway than many other countries. In particular for these other countries one may wonder who is going to pay the bill. The answer is simple: the taxpayer, but then the next question is how and when? But why is it that the rules of fiscal prudence don't seem to apply anymore in today's situation?

And, finally, was not the market supposed to function and to correct itself, possibly at the cost of a certain amount of adjustment pain? The *general* answer to that question is (or was?) yes, but apparently it doesn't work at all times and an extraordinary situation calls for extraordinary measures. That would mean and today's practice seems to suggest that large-scale government interference, including direct fiscal injections, in the economy is all of a sudden accepted again and so are large deficits (it is difficult to see how governments could avoid large deficits at the present scale of spending). That governments do have a role to play when it comes to providing a stable macro-economic framework and healthy monetary conditions is not new insight. But speed and scale at which governments have moved these last few months and shovelled money out, very often in parallel, was unthinkable only a few months ago. Are we seeing a complete revision of economic theory and at least of economic policy?

There is a risk that analysts and policy makers are over-reacting, or "overshooting". After first being too optimistic they may overdo it once again and be too pessimistic this time. Could German Chancellor Angela Merkel be right — and she is not entirely alone — when she claimed that throwing money, borrowed and freshly printed, at today's problems is precisely what caused the crisis? After all, the former chairman of the US Federal Reserve Board, Alan Greenspan, is blamed for contributing to today's crisis among others by lending money at interest rates which were way lower than inflation. In doing so he may have helped pump up the bubble. After all, one side of the crisis is China's over-production the other side is America's excessive spending.

Monetary authorities in the US look for their policy analysis at *actual* inflation as measured by the Consumer Price Index, the CPI. As the US Federal Reserve Board peeked at and followed every move of this CPI, it didn't see inflation emerging and took therefore a lax policy stance and, consequently, allowed excessive liquidity to inflate the prices of houses and other assets. European monetary authorities look in addition at the overall liquidity in the system. The technical name of this liquidity measure, which represents "money and near money", is M3 ("Money Three"[108]). European monetary authorities

---

[108] M1 = coins and banknotes (cash); M2 = M1 + immediately available deposits (cash plus money in the bank); M3 = M2 + time deposits and other instruments which can easily and without costs or risk turned into money.

consider a build-up of liquidity as reflected by an increase in this M3 as a build up of inflation potential or inflation risk, also if it does not apparently translate into higher inflation. American monetary author-ities don't take signals from the liquidity measure M3 into account and, somewhat surprisingly, even stopped publishing M3 data since March 2005.

To get back to those who are sceptical about today's stimulus packages, they do have a point in arguing that it has been reckless spending rather than thrift that caused the crisis. The bubble that has artificially been pumped up should therefore finally be deflated, grad-ually perhaps, is the reasoning of those who reject today's largesse of governments. If they are right the rescue plans should be seen as nothing but extra doses of drugs for a hopelessly addicted economy. It would mean that after earlier bubbles with the housing bubble and the raw material bubble as the latest ones fiscal and monetary stimu-lus would only lead to new and possibly greater problems further down the road. We may reflect on the words of Japan's Economic and Fiscal Policy Minister, suggesting that we may be in a situation of general over-production:

> In my home, if someone asks me "What do you want to buy?"...it would take a week to think. I have a car, two refrigerators, three TV's ... So it is very, very difficult." Such a downbeat view about the prospects for stimulative efforts will be grim news for those observers in western nations who see stronger Japanese con-sumption as a potentially vital part of any early global economic recovery.[109]

Could we be in a situation of fundamental over-production in the Marxist sense and could, in the end, all these stimulus packages lead to nothing lasting? In three or five or ten years from now we may know the answer. Government actions in most countries, but not all,

---

[109] M. Dickie, D. Pilling, Japan shuns role as leader of recovery, *Financial Times*, 2 December, 2008.

go into the same direction, let us hope this is the right direction. In fact, I believe it is. There is hope that the meeting of the G20, the twenty plus richest countries in the world, on 15 November, 2008, in Washington, may later be seen as a turning point in economic policy making. There is hope that meeting shows us that the notion that greater coordination and cooperation are needed is sinking in and lasting. In Europe Euro nay-sayers show a sudden interest in joining the Euro bloc. The Euro has considerably reduced the exposure of small flourishing economies such as the Netherlands and Belgium and also of less healthy ones such as Italy and Greece, demonstrating the point that international coordination and cooperation pay off and are in fact the only option.[110] The G20 meeting of 15 November confirms the point and gives hope that the US finally can agree again that international cooperation is the only option, be a "responsible stakeholder" again.

The US economy, where the crisis started, is particularly hard hit. We read, again, stories about American families of not-so-well educated people, grandparents, children and grandchildren, who practically all depend on automakers or other "old" industries and these industries' suppliers for their living.

> In no other place in Wisconsin factory workers earn as much as here, which has led to a lower than average level of education. Because, why would you bother to get a better education? When General Motors leaves the town next month thousands of unskilled will leave behind. But they do have a big house, two cars and two boats.[111]

Those same autoworkers see the entry of "foreign" automakers in the US market as the turning point. But were not US automakers among the first to go global and set up plants abroad, many decades ago?

---

[110] Although the fact that the Italian and the Greek governments pay much higher interest rates than Germany demonstrates that within the Euro zone fiscal adjustment, which may be more painful, has replaced monetary adjustment.

[111] Freek Staps, "A big house, two cars, but no more job" (my translation from Dutch), *NRC/Handelsblad*, 28 November, 2008.

Toyota and other non-American automakers may comparable numbers of in the US as "American" automakers (who produce part of their cars for the US market in Canada and Mexico). The lament reminds me of what I elaborated on in Chapter II.5: the large numbers of low-skilled labour in the USA.

Putting together the plight of low-skilled US automakers and the difficulty the Japanese Economic and Fiscal Minister has in choosing something he might need and want to buy: perhaps it is time to for US car manufacturers to change tack and start making cars that can compete on world markets. In the 1980's Chrysler survived with support of the US government. In September 2008, when oil prices were still high and US car manufacturers made a first trip to Washington to ask their government for support, Chrysler announced that its latest model went on sale, another petrol guzzling monster. Crisis apart, could it be that Detroit has simply been producing the wrong cars for more than a decade? If so, the way out might indeed be a "new paradigm". New technologies and "green solutions" as the team that is being established by America's President-elect Obama, propagates.

V.3. No More Scarcities?

This author will have to explain a few things. I assumed — implicitly perhaps but I did — that the prices of oil and other resources would remain high. But today many of these prices are less than half of those a few months ago. When the price of a barrel of oil fell below 50 US dollars, in November 2008, market analysts should have jumped up and down with joy, but most comments expressed concern. Even the reaction of consumers was not very upbeat. Why? Lower oil prices today may, at first sight, look like a good thing, but the forces that drive oil prices lower are the forces of crisis and economic decline, which is not something people feel happy about. The world has seen this before. The high oil prices earlier this year had the advantage of at least and finally bringing a variety of alternative energy sources within reach by making them profitable from oil from tar sands to wind energy and other alternative sources. The good news among the bad news about continuously rising oil prices was that finally environmental concerns were taken seriously. The good news in Spring 2008 was that in the United States of America finally sales of SUVs were sharply down and drivers started reducing mileages.

However, with oil prices steeply falling exploration plans and research projects have been shelved where they will be kept waiting until the next oil boom. Investment projects are put on hold, keeping down the potential for greater supply either of oil or alternative energy sources. Existing technologies which can compete with oil when the price of oil is 70 or 80 or 100 US dollar a barrel will no longer be considered when that price is 50 US dollar or lower. Only a few months ago the game was to guess how high the price of oil and other energy sources could go ("oil at US$200 a barrel before the end of 2008"). Today the guessing is how low prices may go. Oil prices may be back at 100 US dollar per barrel once economies have recovered, but who would dare to predict? Moreover, the steep fall from peek prices may be impressive, but prices of oil and other resources are still some 50 percent higher than four years ago. Although I should add that this is true for prices in US dollars, expressed in Euros, prices of resources are practically back at where they were in 2000. So what should be our standard?

What about the rest of my "Malthusian" doom scenario? Not only oil prices have come down, but so have prices of other resources. May the world have steered away, once again, from Malthusian doom and a resource clash, as it did in the 1970's? The more important lesson for all, expressed in the quote above from the "Daily Reckoning", may be that we should be more modest in pretending what we know. This concerns in particular these short and medium term swings. It is good to remember that these recent developments concern the short-term only, call it the *weather*. The story of this book is mostly about the long-term "*climate*", i.e., structures and long-term developments, not about short-term temporary change. Today's storm — the financial havoc and the economic havoc that followed — heavy as it may be, doesn't mean that there is a change in the long-term "climate".

The more long-term patterns, as once again expressed in the four bullet points at the beginning of this chapter, show much greater stability and continue to hold (I believe, let me add this qualifier).

In the following I will put the narrative of the previous chapters in the perspective of today's crisis. I will follow the same order in which I deal with my main issues in the previous chapters. So I will proceed as follows:

- Review economic prosperity and governance and the right institutions in the light of the crisis. How may today's crisis, originating in the West, relate to flaws in the economic policy architecture of the West?
- See how today's crisis relates to what is dealt with in Chapter II, International Competition and Trade
- And finally, ask the question what the crisis means for environmental concerns and sustainable growth

V.4. Good Governance: What Is "Good"?

Today's crisis is to a large degree related to "governance" and domestic factors. It is almost surprising that China hasn't been blamed more for the mess. China has, in the last decade, been unduly blamed for many of the West's ills. And China's overcapacity and continuous current account surpluses and the related imbalances have contributed to the difficulties we are facing today. Perhaps the finger pointing has still to begin.

Today's consensus or "conventional wisdom" is that the crisis, which has contaminated practically all sectors of the western economy and increasingly the rest of the world economy, was triggered in the financial sector of the US with sub-prime mortgages, i.e., mortgage loans to borrowers with insufficient means or credentials. The next step was that these shaky loans were packed together under fancy names and then sold to naive investors, including a multitude of well-reputed banks, who were impressed by the fancy names of the dubious certificates they were buying and had no clue of the risks involved. With cheap money available investors borrowed heavily to be able to buy ever more of these high-risk certificates.

True, greed and recklessness played their role, but greed and recklessness are not new, they have always been there. Greed, recklessness and dubious certificates could prosper because regulation and oversight were insufficient. What happened came down to large-scale gambling in financial markets and once the gamblers were found out it appeared they had taken the system hostage. Because of the essential function of the financial system — "the oil that greases the wheels of the world production machinery" — governments saw no other possibility than to pay the ransom by way of multi-billion dollar/Euro emergency plans.

In the first chapter, where we review the drivers of economic growth, we looked at the importance of "good governance" and proper institutions for the long-term growth and prosperity of nations/economies. High living standards in the West give reason to assume that western institutions are "the best" and should be used as an example and of "best practices" followed. These institutions produce the best results after all — the highest living standards. Remember the good governance indicators of the World Bank and Kishore Mahbubani's "seven pillars of Western wisdom"? When you want to climb up the ladder, follow the West.

In the area of economic policy the set of "best" institutional rules and practices the list of do's and don't's is loosely labelled the "Washington consensus". American economist John Williams coined the term in a paper published in 1989. These rules and practices involve among others fiscal discipline, trade liberalisation, liberalisation of inward foreign investment, privatisation, deregulation and property rights. William's label refers to both the Washington of the US administration and the Washington of World bank and the International Monetary Fund. This so, because, as Williams pointed out in his article, this Washington consensus, initially considered the standard recipe or best practice for rich countries, had become the standard for developing economies too: "Of course, acceptance as relevant to the developing world of ideas that had long been motherhood and apple pie in the developed world was a momentous change."[112]

---

[112] "A short history of the Washington consensus, John Williamson, in N Serra and JE Stiglitz, *The Washington Consensus Reconsidered*, 2008.

Liberalisation and deregulation imply that government's hand should not lay too heavily on the economy, irrespective whether the economy is developed or developing. Regulation on business — "economic agents pursuing profit seeking" — should be limited to the extent possible. It depends on one's ideological orientation whether the emphasis is on "limited" or "possible" and where between the two words one ends up. The world economy has gone through (roughly) three decades where in varying degrees the emphasis was increasingly on "limited". In such a climate calls for stricter regulation and against excessive risk taking and leverage on financial markets were less well received. "The main factor driving the crisis was lack of oversight. And it was international competition between financial centres which led regulators to relax the rules."[113] Or in the words of Jean-Claude Trichet, president of the European Central Bank (ECB):

It was as if we had been keen on eliminating a number of airbags from the car. Yet, now that we have an accident, we are surprised to see that we have a lot of scars [....] Mr. Trichet is clear that global capitalism has been driven in a reckless fashion and that it is time for policymakers to re-read the highway code.[114]

Alan Greenspan, who presided over the Federal Reserve Board until 2005, lectured that markets should be left to themselves and not hindered by too much oversight. As late as in April 2008, as the crisis was unfolding, he commented that markets knew best. Only in September 2008, in the midst of the financial storm, he admitted that he was "shocked" by the lack of responsibility of bankers whom he had presumed to be capable to self-correction. It seemed "overdue", this comment from a seasoned banker and regulator who had been too optimistic about those he had to police. When the former chairman expressed his "shock", governments worldwide were already moving in on a large scale to repair the damage done.

---

[113] Head of Dutch Financial Market Supervisory Body (AFM) H Hoogervorst, on Dutch TV, 7 December, 2008.
[114] R. Atkins, L. Barber, In the face of fragility, *Financial Times*, 15 December, 2008.

There was a strong ideological drive behind the three decades of deregulation, but also thorough analysis and clear evidence. Arguably the US is the world's most deregulated economy and at the same time has achieved the highest living standards in the world, not by coincidence. Leaving aside today's recession woes in the US, continuous huge income inequalities, large-scale poverty, injustice and environmental destruction — the United States of America remains one of the world's most impressive economic success stories. And if that isn't enough, or even more so, we can point at the recent successes of the former communist countries, from Eastern Europe to China, which have demonstrated what, can be achieved when markets are allowed to work. Ronald Reagan's "revolution" in the US in the 1980's was a modest operation compared with Deng Xiao Ping's revolution of "opening and reform" in China, launched around the same time. The "Thatcher revolution" and "Reagan revolution" are shorthand for doing away with the last remainders of "old-fashioned" industrial policy and government intervention in the economy, to be more precise in the west and even more specifically in the UK and the US. There is the notion that continental Western Europe and Germany, in particular, have had their own more regulated, more "social" form of capitalism.

But undue admiration for the Thatcher or Reagan revolution would ignore the fact that focused and specific industrial policy by governments helped bring prosperity to Japan, Taiwan, South Korea and Western Europe. In addition, the important role governments play in large areas of the economy, also in fully developed market economies, is easily overlooked. Take health care, energy, transport infrastructure, education and public transport, all of which account for considerable parts of the GDP and are to different degrees subject to government intervention and various forms of participation by the government, depending which country we look at. The lesson from today's banking crisis is that there should be more regulation, but to what extent? When is regulation not enough, when is it too much?

America's health care system and France's are very differently organised. The French system is much more government financed and led than the American, but (or and?) is considered superior in its *on average* delivery of services. America's market-led health care is, I have little doubt, likely to be superior when it comes to delivering top services to wealthy patients. But France's health care is praised and with good reason for delivering excellent services throughout, to the whole population. Similarly, the more market-oriented education system in the US (than in Europe) is superior in delivering top quality at the top, but the Western European system is superior in delivering average, all right quality on a large scale. In the US the large gaps in the health care system — 45 million people, 15 percent of the population of the richest nation on earth are not insured — are a constant in the political debate of the last two decades. A solution is urgently needed, but also in the richest state on earth it is not a quick fix and the "good governance" and "best practices" debate is going on.

Developments in China demonstrate also that there constant debate is going on and assessment and gradual reform through trial and error take place to move China to, how will I put it, perhaps "closer to the middle ground? In the last few years China has adopted pieces of legislation which can be seen as landmarks for giving a greater role to the market. China adopted laws on competition policy and bankruptcy. Even if we consider that these laws are still incomplete, in particular in the way they actually function (as the implementation mechanisms are not all in place yet) they bring significant changes and are important stepping stones in the building of a market economy although the attention in the western media was modest. Even more important perhaps was the decision in October 2008, that farmers could trade their rights to till the land (which are thirty year leases). It seems another landmark change.

As a move in the opposite direction and in spite of the overall drive for deregulation and liberalisation, in the US the Sarbanes/Oxley bill was adopted in 2002. The law meant a strengthening of financial regulation, in particular, to protect investors after corporate scandals, among them Enron. Opponents complained that the law was too strict and would take away America's competitive edge on international financial markets. After the "financial tsunami" of 2008 one would think the law should have been stricter and the criticism was hollow. The signs are that today's turmoil will in the west lead to a further swing of the pendulum, more so in the US, back to more and stricter regulation and more government intervention.

Would the American people consider that for the moment economic individual liberty has been pushed too far at the cost of the common good? Under its new president the US may find a way to settle its struggle with the flaws in its health care system, its transport infrastructure and perhaps even its secondary education. The ongoing discussion — within and between nations — on how to deal with environmental protection and climate change, it is all related in that it is all about "good governance".

"On the other hand",[115] over-regulation can strangle and kill economic initiative. In the 1980's and 1990's financial markets worldwide were deregulated. Also labour markets, in particular in Europe, were increasingly deregulated so as to create greater flexibility and "release market forces". Labour market policy measures in Europe, most consistently introduced in the northern EU, led to higher employment growth and economic growth in the EU's northern Member States (in particular the Nordic countries, the UK and the Netherlands). But at the same time it is agreed that insufficient regulation of financial markets in the west contributed to today's crisis. And China's very cautious approach towards the liberalisation of its financial market is today considered a blessing as it is generally believed that caution has spared the country greater trouble.

So when is regulation good or just enough? It may sound very boring and discouraging, but it looks like we are back at square one, back at the first chapter where we reviewed governance indicators and the conclusion was that "institutional guidance is meagre". Recent events in world financial markets and the recession will not miss their effect on ideas about "best practices", for instance, in those places in the world which were pressurised to follow the "Washington consensus". Back in the 1990s when Asia suffered from a severe financial crisis, Western governments and institutions told Asian governments under no circumstances to bail out their banks. But now Western

---

[115] US President Truman would have asked for a "one-armed economist", because, he complained, economists advising him always gave two views "on the one hand and on the other".

governments do bail out their own banks. So how strict is the doctrine, what is the best policy to follow Asian governments wonder. The lesson from today's events may be that one should never automatically take from the West's social economic toolbox or from any toolbox for devising a policy. In the first chapter we saw how Poland benefited from "shock therapy reform", but China's leaders stick to gradualism and stress the step-by-step approach at each corner they turn.

What may be the implications of today's crisis for that major challenge we are faced with, i.e., the environmental implications of further world-wide economic growth? The economic crisis of 2008 is likely to last for another year, maybe for a few more years to come. In the context of my narrative the main question then is if, or to what extent, it may affect our rather dim environmental prospects. Environmental researchers remark that the losses suffered during the financial crisis and which are compensated by large sums of government support, are not larger than the damage done to the environment *every year*. As it goes, this environmental damage is so far less directly felt and not immediately showing up in anybody's cashbook. Compare it with the rot developing and building up in the world's credit markets over the years before it came to the surface and brought the roof of the world's financial system down. The day may come that we regret the lack of stricter environmental regulation now as much as we regret today the insufficient oversight of financial markets in the last few years.

V.5. The Environment, International Cooperation

In *Hot, Flat and Crowded*, Thomas Friedman tells us how he, inspired by a talk with the CEO of General Electric, Jeffrey Immelt, reflects on the possibilities for a genuinely forward looking energy policy in the US "if only" the United States of America "could be China for a day" ("but not for two", he adds). During that one day the President could set the right, strategic long-term goals for an energy policy from the top. Friedman quotes Immelt as saying: "I think if you asked the utilities and big manufacturers in this business what they most like, it would be for the president to stand up and say: "By 2025 we are going to produce this much coal, this much natural gas, this much wind, this much solar, this much nuclear, and nothing is going to stand in the way." After his conversation with Immelt, Friedman cannot but envy China's possibility to "cut through all their legacy industries, all the pleading special interests [....] and simply order top-down the sweeping changes in prices, regulations, standards, education, and infrastructure that reflect China's long-term strategic national interests — changes that would normally take Western democracies years or decades to debate and implement."[116]

Friedman uses the telling example of how, in China, the free-of-charge distribution of plastic shopping bags was banned overnight ("Bam! Just like that — 1.3 billion people, theoretically, will stop using thin plastic bags"). However, real life is more sophisticated, complicated and frustrating than in this daydream of Thomas Friedman, even in China. China may not be a one-person-one-vote-democracy, but also China has its decision-making machinery. This machinery is much less explicit and transparent than government structures and processes in the West and it is also less complicated. China's National People's Congress is not the real decision maker. It is sometimes compared with a parliament, but has very limited real power and is in western media usually referred to as "China's rubber stamp parliament". But important strategic policy choices, for instance, about oil prices, energy subsidies and the exchange rate, are reviewed and discussed in China's State Council, and more long-term policies in the Party School. It is a debate of which very little transpires to the outside world, but there is debate, nevertheless.

The irony of Friedman's reflection is that the US and the world probably should consider themselves very lucky that the US was and is *not* China for a day, at least, was not with the president it has had from early 2001 to early 2009. There is little sign that that president would have put in place a healthy energy policy had he had a magic wand. In the last eight years an ever increasing number of Americans have grown much greener than their president. President Bush made

---

[116] T. Friedman, *Hot, Flat and Crowded*, 2008.

the most minimalist effort to push measures that would serve America's long-term energy needs or help fight climate change, as Thomas Friedman seems to assume any American president would. It is the reason why American states and cities have increasingly sought to develop energy policies and action of their own.

The European Union, often derided for its arcane and tedious decision-making mechanisms, has managed to define a relatively consistent, albeit it not yet complete, energy policy for 2020. True, it took tedious, democratic processes and difficult negotiations, but it has. Also, the European Union, again not world famous for its decisive power or capacity to lead the world has played a leading role in the fight against climate change. It has put that fight on top of its agenda and incessantly sought for cooperation with a growing "coalition of the willing". While the US under George W. Bush stayed idle, the EU has continued its lead role in maintaining climate change on the international cooperation agenda, sought cooperation with other more forward looking industrial nations and by doing so set an example.

It is sad and exasperating that today there is only one highly industrialised nation, which hasn't ratified the Kyoto Protocol, the United States. The Kyoto Protocol was signed by Bush's predecessor Clinton, but the former didn't find it worth to fight for it in and, admittedly, not very enthusiastic, Congress (although it might have been a more worthy cause than, for instance the war in Iraq). In spite of Thomas Friedman's noble, but I am afraid, naive suggestion, it seems unlikely that Mr. Bush would ever have declared the Kyoto Protocol valid had America been "China for a day".

Only and finally in 2008 Mr. Bush was prepared to support the view that emissions, including American ones, may have something to do with climate change. Had America subscribed to the Kyoto Protocol, it would have committed to a reduction of emission of 7 percent between 1990 and 2012. Instead, American emissions have increased by 14 percent since 1990. President-elect Obama's objective is to have annulled those 14 percent by 2020. This may sound ambitious, but signing up to Kyoto would have meant that America's annual emissions would in 2020 have been 25 percent below their 1990 level.

And some climate experts think that that this 25 percent is, by far, not ambitious enough. Ambitious experts also think the European Union, the most ambitious Kyoto signatory so far, should and could aim at reducing annual emissions by 40 percent in 2020 (compared to the 1990 basis). Once again, and however ambitious these goals may seem, it is all about *adding less*, but still adding, every year to what is already out there and causing climate change. America's opposition has obviously not been helpful and given the perfect excuse to others to abstain, not least China.

Policymakers in the West and East (and the South and North) should, nevertheless, be credited for keeping the long-term perspective for energy policy and the fight against climate change alive also under the difficult circumstances of the economic crisis and with so little support from the world's most powerful and most polluting state. Fighting the economic crisis has, for the moment, become priority number one, but not at the cost of the fight against climate change (or global warming or our continuous polluting of the environment).

The change of administration in the US, in January 2009, has raised expectations. Thanks to the efforts by the EU, China, in particular, and India, to a certain extent too, have stayed on board of the anti-climate change discussions. China and India haven't been willing to make binding commitments with regard to their emissions, but it is important that they participate in the debate at least and reflect on their future position. And as they do awareness and pressure increase. Today's financial crisis serves as a reminder that we may keep looking away, but the problem stays there:

> In fact, the financial crisis should serve as a warning of the far greater crisis that lies in store unless emissions are cut [....]. The sub-prime risk was something we should have known about, but we ignored it. We know about the risk of climate change. The risk from climate change is substantially larger than the sub-prime risk. Continuing to ignore it will bring us a crisis much greater than we are dealing with now.[117]

---

[117] M. Lubber, quoted in "The heat is on", *Financial Times*, 2 December, 2008.

The occurrence of droughts, storms and floods will increase and in fact is supposed to be already on the rise. The International Energy Agency estimates that until 2050 an extra one trillion Euro *per year* will be needed in investment in green technologies to achieve. That is something of the order of 1.5 percent of the world's national income or the GDP (Gross Domestic Product), each year, which in fact seems manageable. Could it be that today's economic crisis provides an opportunity to address the environmental challenge we are facing, as optimists believe?

> Low-carbon growth encompasses much more than energy efficiency and renewables — it extends to new types of cars and other transport, new building materials and designs, energy transmission systems, new packaging for retailers, the redesign of manufacturing techniques, different farming methods and a host of other developments in nearly all sectors of the economy. This sort of "green growth", on a wide scale, could "lay the foundations of growth for the future", Lord Stern believes. "It is not just a Keynesian pump-up." Looked at correctly, today's economic crisis provides an opportunity to achieve the reformation of the world economy from high to low carbon at a lower cost of action.[118]

For achieving the really substantial reductions in emissions that are required more is needed than just a price on carbon. In addition, regulation will be required, including international coordination of such regulation and subsidies for research. On the minus side are the threat and the ongoing increase of emissions. On the plus side are today's growing awareness and the development of new technologies. A worldwide consensus has still to develop, however as an interview with vice chairman Xie Zhenhua of China's National Development and Reform Commission after the Poznan climate change conference, in December, 2008, demonstrates:

> "The process of negotiations has been rough and failed to meet expectations as the developed countries and their developing

---

[118] Upside of a downturn, *Financial Times*, 2 December, 2008.

counterparts were at odds on their stances on a number of issues," said Xie Zhenhua, Vice Chairman of the National Development and Reform Commission of China [...]. On the core issue of greenhouse gas emission cut targets, Xie said the developed countries are keeping away from making a clear stance. "They are all waiting, especially waiting for the attitude of the U.S. President-elect Barack Obama's incoming administration and that of other major emitters. In fact, they are waiting for others to show their hand," said Xie, head of the Chinese delegation to the Poznan talks. The developing countries, by contrast, have a clear attitude on mission cut target. They insist that the industrialized countries should slash by 25–40 percent of their emissions to the 1990 levels by the year 2020, he said. China suggests that the 25–40 percent target of the developed countries should be a "minimum" amount to leave more room for their developing counterparts. Xie said China and the Group of 77, a bloc of developing nations, have proposed technology transfer as a key measure in the counter-climate change efforts but have only received lukewarm response.[119]

But Xie Zhenhua was not entirely right. China may still be holding off from making commitments for emission reductions. Brazil, Mexico and South Africa did make commitments for such cuts, in a far away future, but commitments nevertheless and Brazil has committed to reduce deforestation considerably.

Pollution in China is rampant and in the West China is generally and rightly perceived as a heavy polluter. The difficulties Beijing had and the struggle it fought to get its air clean and clear during the Olympic Games, the closure of whole manufacturing complexes that was required to achieve that received wide media attention. They formed only one further contribution to China's bad image. Again, that image is well-deserved. Considerable parts of China's population are suffering terribly from the pollution of water, air and soil by manufacturing and power plants, leading

---

[119] Xinhua News Agency, 12 December, 2008.

to widespread disease including various forms of cancer among children.

But among the things China claims is that the international climate change debate should be about *relative* pollution, pollution per person, not only total pollution. In 2005, the fossil fuel use per American was six times what a Chinese citizen used. We saw the figures before, but it is worth repeating: US citizens' use of energy and production of greenhouse gases is more than twice as high as the use of energy and the production of greenhouse gases per citizen in any other rich, developed nation, be it Japan, German, France, the UK or the EU in general. In Russia, not rich, but notorious for its energy inefficiency, energy consumption and greenhouse emissions are half of those in the US.

China and other developing countries conclude that, in spite of their total pollution, pollution per person is still modest compared to what rich countries emit. Why would Americans, Europeans and Japanese be allowed to benefit from their acquired positions and the Chinese and other poor countries not be allowed to "emit as much as they do"? And then, second, account should be taken, they reason, of greenhouse gases released into the atmosphere by developed — let's better be clear and say "rich" — countries over the last two centuries, while these countries were developing. But, as we saw, gradually also developing countries come around and commit to reductions. Reaching international agreement is crucial, but measures should, in the end, be taken at national level. Penalising polluters with trade measures, as a constituency in US Congress is considering (against China in particular), can only lead to counter-measures, a pretext for protectionism and an escalation of animosity.

The international meeting in Poznan, in December 2008, like the meeting one year earlier in Bali, was to prepare the concluding Climate Change Conference, which is to take place from 7 to 19 December, 2009, in Copenhagen. At the Copenhagen conference agreement should finally be reached about environmental goals, clear commitments to reduce emissions, for the period after 2012, when the Kyoto Protocol expires. As usual negotiations are long and difficult. But, aware of what is at stake, participants are open to work on solutions. A key factor is the hoped-for change of attitude of the US administration under a new president. Let us all hope that in one year from now, after the Copenhagen Conference, we can be a little more optimistic about the prospects for the fight against climate change.

References

Anderlini, J. (2008). Beijing prioritises employment for graduates to head off unrest. Retrieved from *Financial Times*, http://www.ftchinese.com/story.php?storyid=001023800&lang=en.

Atkins, R. and Barber, L. (2008). In the face of fragility. Retrieved from *Financial Times*, http://www.ft.com/cms/s/0/7347550a-ca00-11dd-93e5-000077b07658.html?ftcamp=rss&nclick_check=1.

Baldinger, P. (2002). Lean and green: Chinese energy efficiency through ESCOs. World Bank. *China Environment Series 5*, http://wwics.si.edu/topics/pubs/ACF3C9.pdf.

Berstein, W. J. (2008). *A Splendid Exchange*. New York: Atlantic Monthly Press.

Blankert, J. W. (2008). Focus on tech challenge — Not China threat. Retrieved from *Financial Times*, http://www.ft.com/cms/s/0443a75e-2608-11dd-b510-000077b07658.

Bonner, B. (2008). Washington to Detroit: Drop dead! *The Daily Reckoning*. Retrieved from http://www.dailyreckoning.com.au/washington-to-detroit-drop-dead/2008/12/15/.

Bounds, A. (2008). Globalization enriches EU, study says. Retrieved from *Financial Times*, http://www.ft.com/cms/s/96326ff4-e668-11dc-8398-0000779fd2ac.

Brooks, D. (2004). The cognitive age. Retrieved from *International Herald Tribune*, http://www.nytimes.com/2008/05/02/opinion/02brooks.html?scp=1&sq=the%20cognitive%20age&st=cse.

Brown, S. (2004). *Myths of Free Trade: Why American Trade Policy Has Failed*. New York: New Press.

Carson, R. (1962). *Silent Spring*. MA: Houghton Mifflin.

Central Intelligence Agency (CIA). Retrieved from *CIA — The World Factbook*, https://www.cia.gov/library/publications/the-world-factbook/.

Central Party School (2008). Storming the fortress: A research report on China's political system reform after the 17th Party Congress. *Financial Times*, p. 2.

Cody, D. (1987). Corn laws. *The Victorian Web: Literature, History and Culture in the Age of Victoria*. Retrieved from *Wikipedia*, http://en.wikipedia.org/wiki/Corn_Laws.

Dean, J. M. and Lovely, M. E. (2008). Trade growth, production fragmentation, and China's environment. NBER Working Paper, 13860. Retrieved from http://www.nber.org/papers/w13860.

Diamond, L. (2000). A report card on democracy. *Hoover Digest 3*. Retrieved from http://www.hoover.org/publications/digest/3491911.html.

Diana, F. and Jaana, K. R. (2007). How the world should invest in energy efficiency. From www.mckinseyquarterly.com/How_the_world_should_invest_in_energy_efficiency_2165.

Dickie, M. and Pilling, D. (2008). Japan shuns role as leader of recovery. Retrieved from *Financial Times*, http://www.ft.com/cms/s/159d95ac-bfd0-11dd-9222-0000779fd18c.

Dimaranan, B., Ianchovichina, E. and Martin, W. (2007). Competing with Giants: who wins, who loses? In L. A. Winters and S. Yusuf (eds.), *Dancing with Giants*. Singapore: World Bank and the Institute of Policy Studies.

Directorate-General for Economic and Financial Affairs [DG ECFIN] (1994). *Country Studies: Germany*. Brussels, Luxembourg: European Commission.

Dyer, G. (2008). Friction suspends work on Shanghai maglev. Retrieved from *Financial Times*, https://www4.ftchinese.com/tc/story_english.jsp?id=001017795 - 34k.

Dyer, G. and Thornhill, J. (2008). Feeling the heat. Retrieved from *Financial Times*, http://www.ft.com/cms/s/0/133a078e-17e5-11dd-b98a-0000779fd2ac.html?nclick_check=1.

Easterly, W. (2006). *The White Man's Burden: Why the West's Efforts to Aid the Rest Have Done So Much Ill and so Little Good*. New York: The Penguin Press HC.

Economist Intelligence Unit (2006). *Democracy Index*. Retrieved from www.economist.com/media/pdf/DEMOCRACY_TABLE_2007_v3.pdf.

Economy, E. C. (2007). The great leap backward? *Foreign Affairs*, http://www.foreignaffairs.org/articles/62827/elizabeth-c-economy/the-great-leap-backward.

European Commission (2006). EU — China: Closer partners, growing responsibilities. *Communication from the Commission to the Council and the European Parliament*. Retrieved from http://72.14.235.132/search?q=cache:qBTQRw9LNKsJ:www.delchn.ec.europa.eu/download/communication-paper-ENG_070622.pdf.

European Trade Union Confederation [ETUC]. Quality of Jobs at risk! An overview from the ETUC on the incidence and rise of precarious work in Europe. Retrieved from http://www.etuc.org/IMG/pdf_PRECARIOUS_WORK_IN_EUROPEupdate-kh1.pdf.

Flood, C. (2008). Grain production to reach record levels. Retrieved from *Financial Times*, http://www.ft.com/cms/s/b389a42c-1df5-11dd-983a-000077b07658.

Freedom House. (2008). Retrieved from www.worldaudit.org/democracy.htm.

Friedman, T. (2008). *Hot, Flat, and Crowded: Why We Need a Green Revolution — and How It Can Renew America*. New York: Farrar, Straus and Giroux.

Galama, T. and Hosek, J. *US Competitiveness in Science and Technology*. Retrieved from http://www.rand.org/pubs/monographs/MG674/.

Garekar, B. (2008). US manufacturers "don't need protection". From *Straits Times*, p. 8.

GFK (2008). Findings of the GfK consumer climate study From *GFK Group* Web site http://www.gfk.com/group/press_information/press_releases/003754/index.en.html

Ghesquiere, H. (2007). *Singapore's Success: Engineering Economic Growth*. Singapore: Thomson Learning.

Giddens, A. (2007). *Europe in the Global Age*. Cambridge, UK: Polity Press.

Gilboy, G. J. (2004). The myth behind China's miracle. *Foreign Affairs*, from http://www.foreignaffairs.org/articles/59918/george-j-gilboy/the-myth-behind-chinas-miracle.

Giles, M. (2008). The upside of a downturn. Retrieved from http://www.economist.com/theworldin/displaystory.cfm?story_id=12494659.

Greenspan, A. (2007). *The Age of Turbulence: Adventures in a New World*. New York: The Penguin Press HC.

Harney, A. (2008). *The China Price: The True Cost of Chinese Competitive Advantage*. New York: The Penguin Press HC.

Helpman, E. (2004). *The Mystery of Economic Growth*. MA: Harvard University Press.

Hoogervorst, H. (Head of Dutch Financial Market Supervisory Body [AFM]). (2008). In "Buitenhof" on Dutch Public TV, Channel 2.

Hunt, T. (2006). A tale of two cities. *The Guardian*, p. 9; http://www.guardian.co.uk/commentisfree/2006/jul/28/comment.china (for corrections and clarifications).

Hutton, W. (2007). *The Writing on the Wall: China and the West in the 21st Century*. London, UK: Little Brown.

Ikenberry, G. J. (2008). The rise of China and the future of the West. Retrieved from *Foreign Affairs*, http://www.foreignaffairs.com/articles/63042/g-john-ikenberry/the-rise-of-china-and-the-future-of-the-west.

Ikenson, D. (2007). Talk about industry's demise just a manufactured myth. From *Pittsburgh Business Times*, http://pittsburgh.bizjournals.com/pittsburgh/stories/2007/11/26/focus2.html.

IMF Survey Online (2008). Inflation risks have emerged, says IMF's. *IMF Survey Magazine*. Retrieved from http://www.imf.org/external/pubs/ft/survey/so/2008/POL050808A.htm.

Johnson, S. (2008). Enthusiasm for bio-fuels is questioned. Retrieved from *Financial Times*, http://search.ft.com/search?queryText=May+5%2C+2008&aje=true&dse=&dsz=&x=11&y=2.

Kagame, P. (2008). *Africa and Rwanda — From Crisis to Development*. [Public lecture in Singapore].

Kagan, R. (2008). *The Return of History and the End of Dreams*. New York: Knopf Publishing Group.

Kapur, D., Mehta, P. and Subramanian, A. (2008). Is Larry Summers the canary in the mine? Retrieved from *Financial Times*, http://www.ft.com/cms/s/0/19adcdc6-2104-11dd-a0e6-000077b07658.html.

Kaufmann, D., Kraay, A. and Mastruzzi, M. (2007). *On Measuring Government.* www.govindicators: World Bank.

Keefer, P. (2007). Governance and economic growth. In L. A. Winters and S. Yusuf (eds.), *Dancing with Giants.* Singapore: World Bank and the Institute of Policy Studies.

Klein, N. (2007). *The Shock Doctrine: The Rise of Disaster Capitalism.* New York: Metropolitan Books.

Krugman, P. (1996). *Pop Internationalism.* MA: Massachusetts Institute of Technology.

Lubber, M. (2008). The heat is on. In F. Harvey (ed.). Retrieved from *Financial Times*, http://www.ft.com/cms/s/429574ba-b9c4-11dd-99dc-0000779fd18c.

Maddison, A. (2001). *The World Economy: A Millennial Perspective.* Paris: OECD Development Center Studies.

Mahbubani, K. (2004). *Can Asians Think?* Singapore: Marshall Cavendish Editions.

Mahbubani, K. (2008). *The New Asian Hemisphere: The Irresistible Shift of Global Power to the East.* New York: Public Affairs.

Malthus, T. (1798). *An Essay on the Principles of Population.* London: St. Paul's Church-Yard.

Meadows, D. H, Randers, J. L. and Behrens, W. W. (1972). *Limits to Growth.* New York:

Meredith, R. (2007). *The Elephant and the Dragon: The Rise of India and China and What It Means for All of Us.* New York: W. W. Norton & Company, Inc.

Nolan, P. (2004). *Transforming China: Globalization, Transition and Development.* London: Anthem Press.

OECD/PISA. Retrieved from www.pisa.oecd.org.

Olson Jr., M. (1996). Big bills left on the sidewalk: Why some nations are rich, and others poor. *Journal of Economic Perspectives.* **10**(2), 3–24.

Pattis, M. (2008). What China can learn from 1929. Retrieved from *Newsweek*, http://www.newsweek.com/id/174529.

Przeworski, A. and Limongi, F. (1993). Political regimes and economic growth. *Journal of Economic Perspectives.* **3**, 51–69.

Purvis, N. (2008). Narrowing the Transatlantic climate divide. *The German Marshall Fund of the United States.* Retrieved from http://www.euractiv.com/en/climate-change/narrowing-transatlantic-climate-divide-roadmap-progress/article-173712.

Rodrik, D., Subramanian, A. and Trebbi, F. (2002). *Institutions Rule: The Primacy of Institutions Over Geography and Integration in Economic Development.* [Working Paper]. MA: National Bureau of Economic Research.

Sachs, J. D. (2008). *Commonwealth: Economics for a Crowded Planet.* New York: The Penguin Press HC.

Staps, F. (2008). *A Big House, Two Cars, But No More Job* (J. W. Blankert, Translation). The Netherlands: NRC/Handelsblad.

Stephens, P. (2008). Broken banks put the state back in the driving seat. Retrieved from *Financial Times*, http://www.ft.com/cms/s/0/2e754acc-bcb3-11dd-af5a-0000779fd18c.html.

Suyker, W. and de Groot, H. (2006). China and the Dutch economy: Stylised facts and prospects. *Centraal Planbureau, 127*. From http://www.cpb.nl/nl/pub/cpbreeksen/document/127.

The Economist (2008). Poll of the Economist intelligence Unit estimate/forecast. Retrieved from *The Economist*, http://www.economist.com, 2 December 2008.

Timmons, H. (2008). Indians found US at fault in food cost. Retrieved from *International Herald Tribune*, http://www.nytimes.com/2008/05/14/business/worldbusiness/14food.html?scp=1&sq=Instead%20of%20blaming%20India&st=cse.

UNDP (2007). *Human Development Report, 2007/2008*. Available from http://hdrstats.undp.org/indicators.

UNDP (2007). International forum on climate change and science and technology innovation. *Fighting Climate Change: Human Solidarity in a Divided World, 2007/2008*. From http://www.undp.org.cn/modules.php?op=modload&name=News&file=article&catid=13&topic=21&sid=4293&mode=thread&order=0&thold=0

Williamson, J. (2008). A short history of the Washington consensus. In N. Serra and J. E. Stiglitz (eds.), *The Washington Consensus Reconsidered: Towards a New Global Governance*. Oxford, UK: Oxford University Press.

Wolf, M. (2004). *Why Globalization Works*. CT: Yale University Press.

World Bank. (2007). Globalization and inequality. In *World Economic Outlook*. Retrieved from http://www.imf.org/external/pubs/ft/weo/2007/02/pdf/c4.pdf.

World Bank. Retrieved from http://info.worldbank.org/governance/wgi2007/se_country.asp.

Wei Jianhua and Liu Xiang (2008). Chinese Minister: Poznan climate talks pave way for Copenhagen despite failed expectations. *Xinhua News*. Retrieved from http://news.xinhuanet.com/english/2008-12/12/content_10494375.htm

Xinhua (2008). Premier: China stimulus contribution to the world. Retrieved from: http://www.chinadaily.com.cn/china/2009-03/21/content_7603402.htm

Zakaria, F. (2008). Mccain vs. Mccain. Retrieved from *Newsweek*, http://www.newsweek.com/id/134317.

Zakaria, F. (2008). *The Post-American World*. New York: W. W. Norton & Co.

Zakaria, F. (2008). The rise of the rest. Retrieved from *Newsweek*, http://www.newsweek.com/id/135380.

Zoellick, R. (2005). [Speech at the Second US-China Senior Dialogue].

Index